A SURE FOUNDATION

EIGHT TRUTHS
AFFIRMING THE BIBLE'S DIVINE INSPIRATION

DR. DANIEL MERRITT

CROSSBOOKS
PUBLISHING

CrossBooks™
A Division of LifeWay
1663 Liberty Drive
Bloomington, IN 47403
www.crossbooks.com
Phone: 1-866-879-0502

First published by CrossBooks 9/14/2011

ISBN: 978-1-4627-0637-2 (sc)
ISBN: 978-1-4627-0639-6 (dj)

Library of Congress Number: 2011915537

Printed in the United States of America

This book is printed on acid-free paper.

Dedication

THIS BOOK IS DEDICATED to the memory of Goldie Miller Crissman Hobson (1915-2009), whose impact upon so many lives was immeasurable. A faithful member of Richmond Hill Baptist Church, she not only read the written Word, but in her daily life fleshed out the living Word. The Bible was for her a sure foundation upon which she built her life.

Acknowledgment

There are numerous people who have made this book possible. I am most grateful and will always be indebted to the five North Carolina churches that I have served over the last forty years: South Erwin Baptist, Sardis Baptist, Richmond Hill Baptist, Fairview Baptist, and Pleasant Ridge Baptist. Each has given me the privilege to preach the unsearchable riches of Christ, and have allowed me to hone my preaching skills and expand my knowledge of the Bible.

Second, I wish to thank Kari Reeves, Stephen Jordan, and Jim Peterson who helped proof read the manuscript. Each not only proof read these pages; they also made helpful suggestions along the way which were greatly appreciated.

Third, and most importantly, I wish to thank my wife, Shirley, for her patience through all the research and writing. Her understanding and support made it possible for me to put on paper my thoughts stress free. It is hoped that what follows may prove beneficial to those who read it.

Contents

Preface

It has been my privilege to preach from the Bible the unsearchable riches of Christ for over forty years. It has become apparent to me over that period of time that most Christians cannot adequately explain why they believe the Bible to be the inspired Word of God. I have heard said, "I believe the Bible because I have always been taught it is inspired." Others say, "My church, my pastor, or my parents taught me the Bible is inspired by God." Then there are those who will speak from an experiential position and exclaim, "I believe the Bible because it has proven itself to be so in my life." A small minority might say, "I am not sure why I believe it, but I do."

If someone were to ask you why you believe the Bible to be inspired, what would you say? While, of course, faith would ultimately be at the foundation of your answer, could you give an answer that sets forth rational and logical reasons why you know beyond a shadow of a doubt that the Bible is the divinely inspired Word of God? Could you give an answer that would help another Christian affirm their confidence in the trustworthiness and reliability of the Bible? Could you give an answer to an unbeliever that would cause them to give serious thought to the rational evidences that you presented to them?

The purpose of this book is twofold. First, my intent is to give assurance to the Christian that the Bible is without question the inspired Word of God. I want to erase all doubt for someone who might struggle from time to time with the trustworthiness of God's Word. The Christian can be assured the Bible they cherish is divinely inspired. As well, I want to impart information and truths that will enable the

Christian to present challenging arguments to unbelievers who might challenge them as to the Bible's trustworthiness.

Second, my intention is that if an unbeliever reads these pages, there might be enough food for thought contained within that would enlighten them as to the reality of the Bible's inspiration and the message of saving grace found in Jesus Christ. That in essence is the ultimate purpose of this book, to help the Christian to more embrace the Christ the Bible points us to, and to help the unbeliever to encounter the transforming power of Christ. If that twofold purpose can be accomplished my prayers will have been answered.

It is my earnest desire, that each reader may discover for themselves that the Bible has the power to communicate the life of Christ to us mentally, morally, emotionally and spiritually. To honor the Written Word and exalt the Living Word, Jesus Christ, is my aim.

The British preacher Oswald Chambers once said, "In the Bible there is no twilight, but intense light and intense darkness." Whether we dwell in the light or reside in the darkness is determined by our response to the Bible's message concerning Jesus Christ. May this book be an instrument that will aid in Christ's light driving out any darkness of doubt or unbelief that might linger in our hearts.

Daniel Merritt

July 2011

Introduction

This book has been a long time in coming. Its contents have been swirling in my head for many years. Preaching my first sermon as a nineteen year old, on July 4, 1971, I have been preaching the unsearchable riches of Christ for over forty years. For over four decades, on more occasions than I can count, I have had people ask me if it is possible to know for sure if the Bible is truly the divinely inspired Word of God.

When in seminary I had a theology professor who challenged those under his tutelage to know why they believe the Bible to be the Word of God. From that challenge I developed a sermon entitled, "Why I Know the Bible is the Word of God." Over the years I have preached this sermon numerous times. On one occasion, upon the conclusion of the sermon, I had a parishioner remark to me as he was going out the door, "Preacher, you need to write a book about that. Christians need to know how to defend the Bible's truthfulness." That encouraging word planted a seed in my mind and resolve in my soul to someday do as had been suggested to me.

That someday has arrived. Over forty years after preaching my first sermon, which was entitled, "The Need to Get Back to the Bible," there is no doubt in my mind whatsoever that the Bible is the divinely inspired Word of God. In the contents of this book I will share with the reader eight truths that affirm biblical inspiration. One can know with certainty that the Book one holds in their hand is a sure and firm foundation.

I will readily admit that more than any other book, secular or religious, the Bible has drawn intense scrutiny and examination from scholars, scoffers, theologians, philosophers, cynics, the religious, and those seeking a higher meaning to life. Skeptics dismiss the Bible as a book filled with fables and folklore, and even fiction. They scoff at the idea that it is divinely inspired. After all, they contend, the Bible is a human book concocted in the minds of those who are seeking a Power beyond themselves. For the skeptic, reason will not enable one to prove the Bible is anything other than of human origin.

There are others who, even though they are of a more liberal persuasion, are not as harsh in their opinions as the skeptic. They see the Bible's value as only having some good stories that teach moral lessons and principles that will make one's life richer if those principles are followed. Who can argue with the exhortation to love one another and the teaching of Jesus to treat fellow earthly travelers as we ourselves would like to be treated? While such persons may nod in the affirmative to such positive teachings, they are not ready to embrace the Bible as the divinely inspired Word of God.

Then there are those who call themselves Christians, who are conservative theologically, who see the Bible as God's heavenly revelation to humankind. They see the Bible as the inspired, infallible, and inerrant Word of God, being sufficient for faith, daily living, and the extending of hope after this life is over. Those in the conservative theological camp see the Bible as true and vehemently defend its trustworthiness and the veracity of its contents.

Is the Bible fiction, fables, or fact? Is it possible to answer the critics who dismiss the Bible's claims? Is it possible to defend the Bible which has been under such violent attack for centuries? For the skeptic, the agnostic, the atheist, the philosopher, the theologian, or the church member who sits in the pew every Sunday, are there any compelling arguments that can be presented that affirm the truthfulness of the Bible as being the divinely inspired Word of God?

In order to have greater understanding regarding biblical inspiration, let the reader know that extensive background information will be first developed and built upon to develop a more thorough foundation. After examining these foundational aspects regarding biblical inspiration, it will be purpose of this book to present eight compelling truths that affirm the Bible as God's divinely inspired Word to humankind.

The book is divided into two parts. The first part is comprised of the first three chapters. The first chapter will lay a preliminary foundation of three philosophical and theological camps' viewpoint regarding biblical inspiration. So before arriving at our ultimate destination, it is necessary to begin by walking through a minefield of intellectual opinions concerning the Bible which will shed light upon how thinking about the sacred Book has varied and developed. Hang in there through chapter one, and I promise you will be rewarded with an expanse of understanding that will bring rejoicing to your soul, affirming you hold in your hands a divinely inspired Book that is an eternally firm and sure foundation on which you can rest your life and soul.

In chapter two there will be an examination of what the Bible claims about itself regarding inspiration. In chapter three there will be an examination of witnesses from within the Bible and witnesses down through history as to their position on biblical inspiration.

Part two, chapters four through eleven, we will examine eight rational truths that are most compelling in affirming the divine inspiration of the Bible. Each of the eight will be examined and expanded upon, each verifying the truth that there are reasonable arguments that attest to Scripture being more than product of man's wisdom, but a Book that has been inspired by a Divine Mind.

A conclusion will seek to examine faith versus reason as it relates to the acknowledgment and acceptance of the Bible as being divinely inspired; summarizing if the stated purpose of this book has been reached and the importance of the call issued forth from the Bible to all humanity.

Come let us reason together.

PART I
LAYING A FOUNDATION

"This hope we have as an anchor of the soul, both sure and steadfast."

Hebrews 6:19

CHAPTER 1
WHO IS RIGHT?

Found in most Protestant hymnals is the hymn, "How Firm a Foundation." The hymn first appeared in print in 1787. It has been credited to various authors, yet it is not clearly known who penned it. While its authorship may be a mystery, the message of the hymn's first verse is clear. It reads:

> How firm a foundation, ye saints of the Lord,
> Is laid for your faith in His excellent Word!
> What more can He say than to you He hath said,
> You, who unto Jesus for refuge have fled?

The song says that our firm foundation is found in the Word of God—the Bible. It is in His excellent Word that we are to rest our faith, hopes, and aspirations. What more can He say to us than that which He has said in His Word? It is in His Word that humanity finds the hopeful message that a Savior, a Redeemer, has invaded time to illuminate for us the eternal truths. It is in the written Word and the living Word, the hymn proclaims, that humanity finds a foundation and a refuge.

To be sure, the hymn makes a powerful claim. It makes the claim that the Bible and its message of Jesus are a foundation that is secure, sound, and sure. What a claim! Can such a claim be substantiated?

In regard to that question, opinions vary. There are those who say such trust in the Bible is naïve but to each his own. Others will say it is all a bunch of nonsense and the Bible is not to be believed; after all, it is a book of fables and fiction. Then there are those whose hearts burst forth in assurance and passionate praise believing the words of that old hymn to be true.

The Bible is a firm and sure foundation. There are those who see such a statement as one of affirmation ending with an exclamation point. Others see it as a rhetorical question.

The Bible is a firm and sure foundation. Some would wax eloquently in their denouncement or defense of that statement; others would say that there is just no way anyone can ever know one way or the other.

Who is right?

As one journeys back through time, one will find there has been no book that has stirred more debate than the Bible. What have been some of the findings of those from the past who have sought to render a verdict upon the Bible? As shall be seen, there certainly has been no shortage of opinions and views.

What Skeptics Say

There have always been philosophers skeptical of biblical truth that question and seek to arrive at answers regarding life's soul-searching purposes, ideals, and meaning. While many writers from the camp of skepticism could be cited, three representative's views of the Bible will be examined.

David Hume

One philosopher whose writings crossed over into religious speculation was David Hume (1711-1776). His crossover into philosophical theology widely influenced others after him to do so as well.

Born in Scotland, he was raised in a Calvinist environment. While Calvinist teachings held to the divine inspiration of Scripture, Hume shed his Calvinist roots early in life. Though he never totally denounced the possibility of the existence of God, he was undeniably an agnostic. His writings on the Christian faith and dogma were expressions of his skepticism.

Hume saw religious faith as that which is born out of ignorance, and since ignorance is its basis, religious faith is dismissed as superstition.

In his work, *The Natural History of Religion* (1757), Hume attacked inspiration and religious biblical principles declaring, "You will scarcely be persuaded that they are anything but sick men's dreams . . . little more than a repudiation of all superstition."[1]

If the Bible is divinely inspired, it would require a miracle for it to be transmitted between God and man, and Hume surmised that a miracle could never be proven to be the foundation of a system of religion. Hume contended that to defend the Bible and Christian doctrine "is a sure method of exposing it to put it to such a trial as it is by no means fitted to endure."[2] He concluded that, in regard to the Christian faith, it could not be believed by any reasonable person. Faith and reason, for Hume, were incompatible.

Thomas Paine

Though Hume's writings were unsettling to those of his day, he emboldened other skeptics who followed him. One such man, who was just as insistent in his skepticism as Hume, was a leading figure in the American Revolution: Thomas Paine (1737-1809).

Born in England, Paine sailed across the Atlantic to Philadelphia in 1774 at the age of thirty-seven. He is best known for two works: *Common Sense* (1776), and *The Age of Reason*, which was published in three parts in 1794, 1795, 1807.[3] *Common Sense* was a widely spread pamphlet that had a great influence on the American colonists by urging them to make a choice—either live under British tyranny or continue on with the Revolution. His eloquent and passionate appeal to freedom aptly finds him taking his place among those who were called Founding Fathers.

The positive influence Paine had for the freedom of the American colonists was anything but positive when it came to the Christian faith. In *The Age of Reason,* Paine viciously attacked religion, the Christian faith, and the Bible. His writings were so disturbing that his friend, Benjamin Franklin, urged him not to publish them.

Paine's view of the Bible followed that of Hume. He denied the divine inspiration of the Bible, calling it a book filled with "superstition . . . fabulous mythology . . . a book of lies, wickedness, and blasphemy." Paine concluded that "the Christian system of religion is an outrage on common sense." He labeled those who believed in the Bible's divine inspiration as "Christian mythologists."

In a letter Paine wrote to a friend dated August 15, 1806, he wrote, "As to the book called the Bible, it is blasphemy to call it the Word of God." His venomous and irreverent spewing against Christianity and the Bible shocked readers, yet it influenced those who were looking for reasons to embrace such radical skepticism.

Friedrich Nietzsche

One would think it would be hard to find a skeptic who could be more destructive in his words in denouncing the Christian faith and the Bible than Paine, yet one such skeptic can be found in Germany. His name was Friedrich Nietzsche (1844-1900).

Nietzsche was born into the home of a Lutheran pastor, but his father died when he was five years old. From his earliest years, he was drawn to philosophical thought. By age eighteen, his separation from the Christian faith was complete. Of all the philosophical critics of the Christian faith, none have attacked it with such unrelenting radical hatred as Nietzsche.

Without question, Nietzsche was as atheistic as one could get. He wrote in *Ecce Homo* ("Behold the Man"-1888), "'God,' 'immortality of the soul,' 'redemption,' 'beyond'—without exception, concepts to which I have never devoted any attention or time . . . I do not know by any means know atheism as a result; even less as an event: It is a matter of course with me, from instinct."[4]

In his infamous "parable" entitled, *The Madman* (1882), Nietzsche declares the death of God. He wrote, "'Where is God?' [The madman] cried . . . God's, too, decompose. God is dead. God remains dead."[5] He closes the parable by stating that churches are "the tombs and sepulchers of God."

If God is dead, then Christianity and all that Christianity declares to be truth is dead as well. He writes in *The Birth of Tragedy* (1886):

> Christianity was from the beginning, essentially and fundamentally, life's nausea and disgust with life, merely concealed behind, masked by, dressed up as, faith in 'another'

or 'better' life . . . Christianity came into existence in order to lighten the heart; but now it has first to burden the heart so afterwards to be able to lighten it. Consequently it shall perish.[6]

Nietzsche saw Christianity and the Bible as unworthy of one's attention and support, for, according to him, the Apostle Paul invented his own history of Christianity. In his work *Antichrist* (1888), he states, "Whatever a theologian regards as true must be false . . . I condemn Christianity. I raise against the Christian church the most terrible of all accusations that any accuser ever uttered."[7] To believe in God and the Bible, he declared, was a crime against life.

Nietzsche's irrational assault on Christianity didn't come without a price. Because of his radical writings, he found himself more and more isolated from acquaintances, friends, and loved ones. In one of his last correspondences, he wrote to his sister, "A profound man needs friends, unless indeed he has a God. And I have neither God nor friend!"[8]

In 1889, Nietzsche was found by a fellow philosophy professor in a state of insanity. He never recovered. He spent his remaining days being looked after by his sister, dying in August of 1900.

While his venomous pen had been silenced, his writings live on, as do the works of Hume and Paine. Hume, Paine, and Nietzsche have arguably had the most impact in influencing skeptics who succeeded them. Their methodology and arguments have served as a foundation for others who seek to discredit the Bible's divine inspiration and the Christian faith.

Are the skeptics right in their assessment of the Bible?

What Liberal Theologians Say

While one expects skeptics to deny the divine inspiration of the Bible, one would expect those who label themselves Christian theologians and ministers to defend its inspiration. Yet in looking at what liberal theologians say about the Bible's divine inspiration, one discovers much of the supernatural aspect of the Bible is swept away in favor of a more subjective, naturalistic Christianity that emphasizes the believer's inward experience.

Friedrich Schleiermacher

The father of Christian liberalism is generally considered to be Friedrich Schleiermacher (1768-1834). Born in 1768, his father was a Prussian army chaplain. Growing up in a home influenced by the Moravian faith and traditions, he entered seminary to study for the ministry. However, his studies developed in him a skepticism that found him breaking with the orthodox Christian faith.

Schleiermacher began to depend less and less on Christian biblical doctrine and dogma, emphasizing one's personal experience as more important. He emphasized that Christianity was a personal relationship with God, downplaying the historical Christian truths as found in the Bible.

His Christianity became more subjective (one's inward experience) and less dependent on the propositional truths of the Bible. It is one's personal experience that inspires the Bible not vice a versa. Schleiermacher contended that one does not believe in Christ because they believe in the Bible, one believes in the Bible because they believe in Christ.

For Schleiermacher the Bible gains its authority from one's faith in Christ, elevating personal experience over the Bible. In *The Christian Faith,* he writes, "The authority of Holy Scripture cannot be the foundation of faith in Christ; rather must the latter [faith in Christ] be presupposed before a peculiar authority can be granted to Holy Scripture."[9] Again, he contended one's personal experience inspired the Bible rather than the Bible being inspired and authoritative regardless of one's experience.

Schleiermacher maintained one of true faith "could most easily do without" a sacred writing. He did not believe in "a special doctrine about these writings, as having had their origin in special divine revelation or inspiration."[10]

He even rejected parts of the Bible as inauthentic, believing "such authority we do not ascribe uniformly to every part of the Holy Scripture."[11] For example, in 1807, he wrote a work seeking to prove that First Timothy was not authentic. Of course, the question is raised that if the Bible is not trustworthy, if parts of it are not divinely inspired, then how can one believe in any part as to what it says in regards to believing in Christ and other Christian truths? What is to be the guide of those who have a personal experience with Christ? If not the Bible, then what is to be one's guide?

Schleiermacher's emphasis on personal experience without giving assent to the propositional truths of the Bible, his elevating subjective experience not dictated by dogma or by the letter of Scripture, is at the heart of his theology and of liberal Christianity. One who follows the theological path of Schleiermacher doesn't need an inspired Bible, as long as the person has an inspired personal experience.

Soren Kierkegaard

Carrying Schleiermacher's emphasis on personal experience above an inspired Bible a step further was the Danish theologian Soren Kierkegaard (1813-1855). He sought to lift faith above reason in one's relationship with God. He taught one's subjective relationship was to be preferred over the objective truth of Christianity. Since the Bible is objective truth, it can actually hinder faith. For the revelation of God cannot be contained in one book like the Bible.

In his work, *The Concluding Unscientific Postscript* (1846), he writes, "Faith is precisely the contradiction between the infinite passion of the individual's inwardness and the objective uncertainty. If I am capable of grasping God objectively, I do not believe, but precisely because I cannot do this I must believe."[12]

On the matter of a subjective faith over the truth of objective truth (the Bible), he writes:

> The passion of the Infinite is precisely subjectivity, and thus subjectivity becomes the truth. Only in subjectivity is there decisiveness; to seek objectivity is to be in error. It is the passion of the infinite that is the decisive factor and not its content, for its content is precisely itself. In this manner subjectivity and the subjective 'how' constitute the truth.[13]

If Kierkegaard's logic is to be followed, that in subjectivity is truth, then there is little need for an inspired Bible. His emphasis on inward subjectivity over objective revelation, over the historical basis of faith, gives little regard to the objective side of truth as found in the Bible.

While, for Schleiermacher and Kierkegaard, the Bible may have a place in the Christian life, it is not of supreme importance or even altogether necessary, as one's subjective (inward) experience is more important than a divinely inspired Bible.

Rudolf Bultmann

A twentieth-century theologian who went even further than Schleiermacher and Kierkegaard when it came to divorcing the objective truth of the Bible from one's subjective experience was Rudolf Bultmann (1884-1976). Born in Germany, he was a New Testament theologian, who in 1941, introduced to the theological world the word, demythologization (removing the myths).

Bultmann's interpretive method of demythologizing the New Testament was to strip away from the stories, events, and people all that was cloaked in mythology. James C. Livingston says that for Bultmann, "The New Testament drama of redemption is pictured in an elaborate cosmological and eschatological myth."[14]

In his lectures on *Jesus Christ and Mythology*, given in 1951 at Yale and Vanderbilt and later published, he writes:

> The whole conception of the world which is presupposed in the preaching of Jesus in the New Testament generally is mythological; i.e. the conception of the world as being structured in three stories, heaven, earth, hell; the conception of the intervention of supernatural powers in the course of events; and the conception of miracles, especially the conception of the intervention of supernatural powers in the inner life of the soul; the conception that men can be tempted and corrupted by the devil and possessed by evil spirits. This conception of the world we call mythological because it is different from the conception of the world which has been formed and developed by science.[15]

For one to get to the real Jesus of the New Testament, according to Bultmann, one must strip away all the mythology. In history past mythology had many versions of "saviors." What is the difference between Jesus and other ancient saviors? James Kay answers, "[For Bultmann] the difference between the New Testament and other ancient versions of dying and rising saviors is that the New Testament 'intertwines' its Christ figure with a real historical person, Jesus of Nazareth, who was crucified under Pontius Pilate."[16]

Bultmann believed that true faith is not built on a foundation of historical facts as found in the Bible, but in hearing and acting upon the message of Christ. Only when one demythologizes [wades through all the myths] can the New Testament message be heard. Such a faith will be a subjective faith, not based upon on an inspired Word of objective truth.

Schleiermacher, Kierkegaard, and Bultmann's writings have had far reaching influence in elevating subjectivity over objectivity in regard to faith and biblical inspiration. It is clear their liberal theology doesn't coincide with the divine inspiration of the Bible. For the liberal theologian, a subjective faith is of higher value than a faith based on the foundation of inspired truth.

Are liberal theologians right in their assessment of the Bible?

What Conservative Theologians Say

How do conservative theologians differ in their view of the Bible as compared to skeptics and liberal theologians? The answer is, much in every way.

John Calvin

One of the first theologians to develop a definitive view on the inspiration of the Bible was John Calvin (1509-1564). Calvin was a second generation Protestant Reformer, coming some twenty-five years after Martin Luther (1483-1546) and Huldrych Zwingli (1484-1531), who had initiated the Reformation.

Calvin's view of the inspiration of the Bible laid a foundation which others, who have followed him, have built upon. His assessment on biblical inspiration is of supreme value. His writings have had an immeasurable influence that still impacts the Church today.

Calvin was born in France into a Roman Catholic home. Becoming a lawyer, he came under the influence of the Protestant Reformation and embraced the Christian faith in the early 1530's. In 1536, he had to flee to Switzerland because of persecution against Protestants. Eventually becoming the spiritual leader of Geneva, he remained so until his death in 1564.

A prolific writer, he is best known for writing the *Institutes of the Christian Religion* (1536). It is a massive systematic work that expounds Protestant faith and doctrine. Found within the *Institutes* is Calvin's view of the inspiration of the Bible.

For Calvin, the Bible is a necessity because without it we have no clear revelation of God or a sure direction in matters of faith and doctrine. Calvin presupposed that this revelation of God found in the Bible was inspired. He writes in the *Institutes*:

> God is its Author . . . The Scriptures are from God, but in a way superior to human judgment, feel perfectly assured as much so, as if we beheld the divine image visibility impressed on it, that it came to us, by the instrumentality of the men from the very mouth of God.[17]

While the personalities of the biblical authors could be seen in their writings, the Holy Spirit overshadowed them as they wrote. There was no doubt for Calvin that in the Bible "that God in person speaks in it."[18] Calvin further adds, "The apostles were the certain and authentic amanuenses of the Holy Spirit, and therefore their writings are to be received as the oracles of God." [19]

As the Holy Spirit's amanuenses, through His supernatural work, "the original writers of Scripture were guarded from all error in matters of doctrine as well as in matters of history."[20] Because of the supernatural nature of the Bible "there is such life energy in God's Word."[21]

Calvin's writings pertaining to the Bible's divine inspiration were much needed. Those of the Reformation who came out of the authoritative Catholic Church needed a "new" authority, and Calvin's teaching on biblical inspiration gave the Reformed churches such a foundation. It is a foundation churches of all denominations still need.

Francis A. Schaeffer

While Calvin was the Lord's instrument in upholding the banner of divine inspiration in the spread of the Reformed Movement, the twentieth-century was blessed with a champion for the sufficiency of Scripture and its inspiration. His name was Francis A. Schaeffer (1912–1984).

Schaeffer, who was born in Germantown, Pennsylvania, accepted Christ at age eighteen. In his education and seminary training he was influenced by and identified with the Presbyterians. A brilliant and analytical thinker, his scholarship and intellectual ability was extraordinary. Upon finishing his studies he pastored for awhile, but in 1948 he and his wife, Edith, moved to Switzerland.

In 1955, he founded a community in Switzerland called L'Abri Fellowship. Schaeffer, a theologian, philosopher, and lecturer, spent his life speaking, writing, and defending the Christian faith against secular humanism and a culture that was in a state of spiritual and moral decay. He was, without question, one of the most influential thinkers of the twentieth-century, writing twenty-five books.

Schaeffer denounced liberal theology and its denial of the Bible as the inspired Word of God. In a letter written to a friend in 1958 he wrote, "Liberalism with its denial of the Bible as the Word of God destroys all possible authority of an absolute nature. Therefore, I feel liberalism is so completely destructive in the finding of the truth . . ."[22] In a 1960 letter he wrote he was praying for a friend to be enabled to grasp "the intellectual reality of that which God is and what God has revealed in the objectively inspired Bible."[23]

Schaeffer's belief in an inspired Bible is diametrically opposed to the liberal theologians who elevate subjective truth over objective truth. He taught it was through the Bible God communicates to humankind. He writes:

> Since God made man to communicate with other men through verbalization; it is not surprising that there is a place for verbal, propositional communication from God to man and from man to God. The Bible claims, the Old and

New Testament together, that the Bible itself is the verbal communication from God to man.[24]

A prolific author, in his 1968 work, *Escape From Reason,* he seeks to analyze the trends of modern thought in relation to the Christian Faith. He has a section in the book entitled, "The Bible Can Stand on Its Own."[25] He contends that though suffering attacks from skeptics and liberals down through the years, the Bible, because of its supernatural nature, is sufficient to stand on its own even in the face of those attacks.

Schaeffer hears the voice of God in the sacred text, "The Bible sets forth its own statement of what the Bible itself is. It presents itself as God's communication of propositional truth, written in verbalized form, to those who are made in God's image . . . [B]oth the secular and the unbiblical theological thinking of today would say that this is impossible. But that is precisely what the Bible says it sets forth." [26]

It is clear to see, Francis A. Schaeffer was truly an intellectual champion when it came to defending the Bible as the divinely inspired Word of God. Though his pen is no longer active, his many writings are available to read for the Christian's stand against skepticism and liberalism.

Billy Graham

In our look at conservative Christians who hold to the Bible as being divinely inspired, it would be remiss to not look at a man whose influential ministry and writings have spanned both the twentieth and into the twenty-first century. That man is Billy Graham.

Graham was born in 1918 in Charlotte, North Carolina, into the home of parents who were dairy farmers. Coming to Christ as a sixteen year old, he later sensed the call of God on his life to enter the ministry. Attending Bob Jones College, then Florida Bible Institute, and then Wheaton College in Illinois, after his graduation in 1943, he pastored for awhile and even served for a time as president of Northwestern College. A Southern Baptist, his booming, clear voice made him a revival favorite.

He began conducting evangelistic crusades in 1948, and in 1950 formed the Billy Graham Evangelistic Association, becoming a full-time conservative Christian evangelist. For more than seventy years Billy Graham has been a name known and respected around the world. A man who is comfortable with a pauper or prince, he has met and prayed with every President since Harry S. Truman.

Preaching the Bible with conviction and without compromise, his views on the Bible are worth examining. An author of numerous books, in his book *The Holy Spirit* (1968), he states:

> God the Holy Spirit inspired the men who wrote the Bible . . . Scripture is literature indwelt by the Spirit of God . . . [While] the Holy Spirit in His work did not bypass the human processes, but instead, He worked through them . . . We do know that He used living human minds and guided their thoughts according to His divine purposes. Moreover, it has always been clear to me that we cannot have inspired ideas without inspired words.[27]

As a conservative evangelist/theologian, Graham holds to inspiration of the words but also to the whole of biblical inspiration. He says, "When we speak of the total (or plenary) inspiration of the Bible, we mean that the entire Bible, not just some parts of it, is inspired."[28] How is that possible? It is possible, according to Graham, who quotes Southern Baptist scholar B.H. Carroll (1843-1914), who said, "The Bible is called holy because it is that infallible, *theopneustos* [God-breathed-out] product of the Holy Spirit."[29]

Graham concludes that since the Bible is inspired, it is also authoritative for humanity. As well, it is authoritative because it is God's revelation to man. We yield to the Bible because it comes from God.

Graham urges the Christian to have confidence in the Bible because, "the same Holy Spirit who was the author of the Scriptures through the use of human personalities, also works in each of us to convince us the Bible is the Word of God to be trusted in all its parts."[30]

Calvin, Schaeffer, and Graham's lives and writings have had far reaching influence on conservative Christians who seek to settle the question of whether or not the Bible is divinely inspired.

Having spent time looking at three influential representative voices from the camps of skepticism, liberal theology, and conservative theology, which one of the three camps are right in their assessment of the Bible?

It is the confident belief of this writer that the conservative theologian is the one who is right in regard to the divine inspiration of the Bible. Before considering the eight truths that affirm the Bible's inspiration the next two chapters will examine the Bible's claim of revelation, inspiration, and authority; historical witnesses; and finally arriving at compelling arguments for the truthfulness of the Bible as being divinely inspired.

In order to grasp and understand the truths contained in the Bible it is of necessity for one to approach it with the presupposition as to what the Bible claims about itself. And just what does the Bible claim about itself?

CHAPTER 2
THE BIBLE'S CLAIM

In the previous chapter we looked at three representative voices from three different camps regarding how the skeptic, the liberal theologian, and the conservative theologian view the Bible in regard to whether or not it is divinely inspired. From a vehement denial as to it being inspired, to a passionate defending its inspiration, the voices of others has been heard. What, though, about the voice from the Bible itself?

Before proceeding, what does the book Christian's call the "Bible" mean? Our English word "Bible" comes from the Greek word *biblos* and *biblion*, meaning "scroll" or "book." The paper on which the Scriptures (as well as other documents) were written was made from papyrus (*byblos*). A roll of papyrus to be used as writing material was called *biblion*. In time the whole of the sacred writings came to be called, "The Book" or the Bible.

What does this "book," the Bible, say about itself? What are the Bible's claims in regard to revelation, inspiration and authority? In answering these questions, testimony from the Bible's own pages is a Voice that begs for humankind to listen.

Let it be known from the outset that the Bible makes a bold claim about itself. It claims to be *theopneustos,* a "God-breathed-out" book (2 Timothy 3:16).

The Bible's Claim Of Being God's Revelation
What is meant by the word "revelation?" Revelation means an unveiling, an uncovering, a disclosure. By the word "revelation" it

is to be understood that some fact or truth about a matter cannot be known unless the veil that shields it is lifted in order that one can know something that has been previously unknown and could not be known unless it was uncovered. Revelation is disclosing something that has before been hidden.

On the need for a revelation, Harold Lindsell writes, "We must emphasize the fact that there are many things we do not know and cannot know in and of ourselves. We can only know them from revelation, that is, from God's disclosure of them to us."[31] The Bible claims itself to be just such a revelation.

The Bible claims to be the revelation, the self-disclosure of God to humanity. According to Carl Henry, to say the Bible is God's revelation to humanity speaks "of God's communication to man of divine truth, that is, His manifestation of Himself or of His will."[32] David Dockery says, "Revelation is God's manifestation of Himself to humankind in such a way that men and women can know and have fellowship with Him."[33]

In defining revelation Lindsell writes, "By revelation we mean that God has made Himself known and this self-disclosure has been inscripturated uniquely in the Bible . . . God, in order for man to find Him, revealed Himself supernaturally [in the Bible]."[34]

The late Augustus H. Strong (1836-1921), eminent Baptist theologian, says that in the Bible, "God has actually undertaken to make Himself known to men."[35] Francis A. Schaeffer writes, "The Bible sets forth its own statement of what the Bible itself is. It presents itself as God's communication of propositional truth, written in verbalized form to those who are made in God's image."[36]

Yes, the Bible claims itself to be God's revelation of Himself to humankind. The Bible claims within its pages God is disclosing truths about Himself that could not be known in any other way unless God chooses to make it known. The Bible containing truths that are eternal and divine are revealed to us because God took the initiative to do so.

All through the Bible we see the internal declaration of God revealing Himself to humanity; making known aspects about Himself that could not be known if He had not chosen to make Himself known. In the fifth book of the Pentateuch these words are recorded, "The secret things belong to the LORD our God, but those things which are revealed belong unto us and to our children forever, that we may do all the words of this law" (Deut. 29:29). (From henceforth all Scripture quotations are taken from the New King James Bible version unless otherwise noted.)

While, no doubt, God has not revealed to man everything about Himself, God has taken the initiative to reveal truths that could not be known unless He revealed them. It behooves humanity to seek to know those truths which He has uncovered that man might know Him.

As one turns to the first book in the Bible, Genesis, one discovers the first four words are, "In the Beginning God . . ." (Genesis 1:1). That God exists is not debated, His existence is presupposed. One will not find any wordy or extensive theological arguments for His existence. The fact of His existence is taken for granted and assumed. From the first words of the Bible God seeks not to prove his existence, but reveal Himself to humankind.

In the very first chapter of the Bible we see the God of Heaven revealing Himself in and through His creative work. We see His self-disclosure in the phrase, "And God said . . . ." (Genesis 1:3, 6, 9, 11, 14, 20, 24, 26, 29)

God said and it was. Dale Moody writes, "God's revelation is, in biblical language, God's word . . . God's word is God's revelation of Himself."[37] By the expressive Word of God, as seen in creation, the Lord began His self-revelation of Himself. David Egner points out, "The Hebrew term translated 'Word of the God' is *deber Yahweh*. A brief study of that phrase in the Old Testament shows that when the Word of the Lord is made known, it comes with authority, wisdom, and specific revelation."[38]

In the first chapter of the Bible, God is giving a specific and special revelation of Himself as a God who creates, who is involved in His creation, who provides for those He created, who desires the fellowship of His creation, and who seeks to perpetually communicate with humankind. God in His creation gave a specific and special revelation of Himself, and found within nature God has unmistakably given humanity a general revelation of Himself that points to Him.

The Psalmist points out the obvious, "The heavens declare the glory of God and the firmament shows His handiwork" (Ps. 19:1). Paul tells us that man can't claim ignorance about the existence of God, "Because what may be known of God is manifest in them, for God has shown it to them. For since the creation of the world His invisible attributes are clearly seen, being understood by the things that are made, even his eternal power and Godhead; so that they are without excuse" (Rom. 1:19-20).

While the general revelation of God through creation is evident, it falls short of telling us much about the character of God other than He is a Supreme Being, an Intelligent Designer. To discover what this Supreme Being is like He needs to give us a special revelation. He did; it is called the Bible. In the Bible, God communicates truth about Himself not known before and could not be known by simply observing nature.

The Bible is a record of God's revelation of Himself to those He created. We see Him revealing and communicating Himself in the Old Testament in many ways. He revealed Himself to Adam as a God who desired his fellowship by talking with him and walking with him in the cool of the day (Genesis 3:8), He revealed Himself through audible voice to Noah as a God who desires man live righteous (Genesis 6:1-13), He revealed Himself through voice and dreams to Abraham as a God who had a purpose that Abraham's descendants would provide a Savior for a sinful humanity (Genesis chapter 12).

We see God revealing Himself in the early chapters of Genesis as a God whose revelation is purposely a redemptive revelation. God reveals Himself for the purpose of communicating to humanity that they have not been left alone to grapple with the problem of sin and evil, but He Himself plans to provide for sinful humanity a redeemer, a Savior. God's communications to man was/is with that redemptive purpose in mind.

The Bible records God revealing Himself in acts of history, stepping from eternity into time to make Himself known. He has revealed Himself in a variety of ways.

He revealed Himself to Jacob in a dream (Genesis 28); He revealed Himself to Moses in the burning bush (Exodus 3:1-6); He revealed

Himself to the children of Israel in the ten plagues and the parting of the Red Sea (Exodus 14); He revealed and communicated Himself to the priests through the Urim and Thummim (Numbers 27:21); He revealed Himself to Joshua in a theophany (an appearance of God in human form) (Joshua 5:13-15); He revealed Himself to Samuel in an audible voice (I Samuel 3); He revealed Himself to Daniel in visions and dreams (Daniel 2, 7-10); He revealed Himself to the three Hebrew children in the fiery furnace as the Fourth Man in the fire (Daniel 3); He revealed Himself to Elijah in a whirlwind (2 Kings 2:1-11); He continually revealed Himself to the nation of Israel through His prophets; and He revealed Himself to the prophets and others in many and different ways (Hebrews 1:1).

As the Lord spoke to His prophets, revealing the message He desired to be shared with His people, that message was delivered by the prophets with a resounding, "Thus saith the Lord . . ." They sought to communicate what the Lord had revealed to them. Another phrase we see occurring throughout the Old Testament is, "The word of the Lord came unto . . ." Occurring some 130 times, it expresses God's initiative to communicate with those He created.

While God is seen in the revelation of Himself in events, people, circumstances, and nature, what was/is the ultimate purpose of His self-disclosure? All through the Old Testament we see God progressively unfolding and revealing more of Himself and His purposes in preparing the world for the One to come who would be the provision for man's sin. God's revelation of Himself and His purposes reaches its apex when at last "when the fullness of time had come God sent forth His Son born of a woman, born under the law, to redeem those that were under the law, that we might receive the adoption of sons" (Galatians 4:4-5).

In the New Testament, God's revelation of Himself culminates in Jesus Christ. In Jesus Christ, the One in whom redemptive revelation supremely resides, one meets the God who revealed Himself in Genesis chapter one. In Christ, God has "made known to us the mystery of his will according to His good pleasure, which he purposed in Christ . . ." (Ephesians 1:9-10, KJV)

That Jesus is God in the flesh, God's dear Son, the promised Savior could and can only be known by divine revelation. When Simon Peter declared Jesus to be the Son of God, Jesus said to him, "Blessed are you, Simon Bar-Jonah, for flesh and blood has not revealed this to you, but My Father who is in heaven" (Matthew 16:16-17). Peter could not have known that truth unless the Father had revealed it to him.

In Christ, in the historical Jesus, one discovers God's revelation of His redemptive purpose. As a God who has chosen to reveal Himself, He reveals Himself in the record of His written Word and He reveals Himself in the incarnate, living Word.

Through the Bible, the written revelation of God, and Christ, the living and incarnate Word of God, He continues to reveal Himself to those who will open their hearts to the Bible's claim of being God's revelation.

It is clear the Bible claims itself to be the divine revelation of God to humanity. If the Bible is God's self-disclosure of Himself, then what about its claim regarding inspiration? The Bible claims to be not only the revelation of God, but it also claims to be the inspired Word of God.

The Bible's Claim To Being Divinely Inspired

Of all the books that have ever flowed from man's pen, the Bible is different from all of them. The Bible claims for itself divine inspiration. Paul wrote to Timothy, "All Scripture is given by inspiration of God . . ." (2 Tim. 3:16). The word translated "inspiration" is *theopneustos*. It is made of two Greek words; *theos,* which means God; and *pnein* which means to breathe. B.H. Carroll translates the word to mean, "God-breathed-out."[39] The Bible declares itself to be the God-breathed Word of God.

It only follows that if the Bible is God's divine revelation then it would be inspired by the One who has revealed Himself. The Bible is not a product of man's wisdom, "but holy men of God spoke as they were moved by the Holy Spirit" (2 Peter 1:21). Peter declares the Bible is an inspired book.

In Romans we find the Old Testament Scriptures called "the oracles of God" (Romans 3:2). As the oracles of God, they were viewed to be not only a revelation from God, but divinely inspired.

What is meant when one says the Bible is inspired? Before looking at what divine inspiration means and what the Bible claims about itself in regard to inspiration, it would prove profitable to look at what inspiration does not mean.

What Inspiration Does Not Mean

First, biblical inspiration is not human genius. When speaking of human genius or human inspiration one thinks of great writers like Shakespeare, Robert Frost, Mark Twain, Edgar Allen Poe, Robert Browning, and Charles Dickens. While their writings are an example of the best of human genius and human inspiration, biblical inspiration is much more than that. The writers of the Bible ranged from farmers like Amos, to the educated, like Paul, and their ability to communicate heaven's message required more than human genius.

Second, biblical inspiration is not simply illumination of the writer. This theory of biblical inspiration holds the writers were subject to degrees of illumination or inspiration in their writings. This theory of inspiration, says Augustus Strong, "regards inspiration as merely an intensifying and elevating of the religious perceptions of the writer."[40] This view devalues the Bible and makes it untrustworthy, as the value of what one reads in the Bible would depend on the degree of illumination the writer had at the time that he penned those particular words.

Third, biblical inspiration is not mechanical dictation. The writers of the Bible were not robots who "channeled" the Holy Spirit, devoid of consciousness or human thinking and personality. The writers were not passive instruments. Their individuality was not ignored by God, but is woven throughout what they wrote. Yet they, at the same time, by God's supernatural influence, recorded what He wanted written.

In inspiration of the Bible, God did not bypass the author's human intelligence and their natural character traits. The writers were penmen not passive pens.

Fourth, biblical inspiration does not remove human personality. In inspiring the authors of the Bible, the Lord used each writer's unique personality, literary style, temperaments, and geographical and educational backgrounds without eliminating their uniqueness. Wayland Hoyt explains, "Inspiration is not a mechanical, crass, bald compulsion of the sacred writers, but rather a dynamic, divine influence over their freely-acting faculties."[41]

Concerning this point, James Draper writes:

> God so supernaturally directed the writers of Scripture that without waiving their human intelligence, literary style or personal feeling, His complete and coherent message to man was recorded with perfect accuracy, the very words of the original Scripture bearing the authority of divine authorship.[42]

As one reads the Bible, it is evident that within the many author's writings they had different literary styles, educational backgrounds, and personalities, and God being a God of infinite variety used each of the writers to express what God would have them to express. While the Lord prepared each writer supernaturally, He did not do away with the uniqueness of who the writer was.

Fifth, biblical inspiration does not mean verbatim quotations and grammatical uniformity among the writers. Those who attack the divine inspiration of the Bible are quick to point out places where a New Testament writer quotes from the Old Testament and they do not quote it verbatim.

A few examples are worth noting. This can be found in James 4:6, where he quotes Proverbs 3:34. James says, "Therefore he says, God resists the proud, but gives grace to the humble." The verse in Proverbs reads, "Surely he scorns the scornful: but he gives grace to the humble."

Another example is found in the book of Peter where he quotes Isaiah 53:9. Peter in speaking of Jesus writes, "Who committed no sin, nor was deceit found in His mouth" (I Peter 2:22). The corresponding passage in Isaiah reads, "Because He had done no violence, nor was any deceit in his mouth" (Is. 53:9).

Citing one more example, found in Hebrews the author quotes from Proverbs 3:12 when he writes, "For whom the LORD loves He chastens, and scourges every son whom He receives" (Heb. 12:6). The verse in Proverbs reads, "For whom the LORD loves He corrects, just as a father the son in whom he delights."

While James, Peter, and the author of Hebrews did not quote verbatim from the Hebrew Old Testament (Masoretic Text) in these texts, they did quote from the Septuagint, which is a Greek translation of the Hebrew Old Testament made between 250 and 150 B.C.

What needs to be realized is that oftentimes, as in the examples cited, the New Testament writer when quoting from the Old Testament quotes from the Septuagint which he is more familiar. The majority of the quotations found in New Testament come from the Septuagint.

Sidney Collett informs, "That out of about 263 direct quotations from the Old Testament, 88 are verbal quotations from the Septuagint, 64 borrowed from it."[43] With the Hellenistic (Greek) influence of the New Testament period, a biblical writer would often be more at home with the Septuagint than the Hebrew Old Testament; as well, most of the readers would be more at home with Greek than Hebrew, so why should it be a surprise they quote from the Septuagint.

As far as grammatical uniformity, rules of grammar would vary from one geographical area to another, meaning that each writer would have their own phrases of expressions unique to them. Again, each writer had different educational backgrounds as well. Those two factors alone would lend one not to expect grammatical uniformity. A lack of grammatical uniformity among all the writers is not to be considered as an argument against inspiration, but is simply the uniqueness of the individual writer.

Sixth, biblical inspiration does not mean that translations or versions are inspired, but the original autographs. When speaking of inspiration of the biblical text, it is the original autographs that are inspired not the many and various translations one can find on the market today.

Critics would contend this is a moot point since we no longer possess the original autographs, but that which has been handed down to us by meticulous copyists. However, with over 5,000 manuscripts that have descended from the *autographa* available for biblical scholars to study and compare, scholars have, for all intents and purposes, restored the original autographs. R.A. Torrey writes, "When all those thousands of documents are checked, compared, combined, grouped, studied, we have certain and final assurance regarding the [biblical] text."[44]

Augustine sought to explain the difference between the original autographs or manuscripts and a translation from those manuscripts that one might be reading.

> I do not doubt that their authors [the biblical authors] therein made no mistake and set forth nothing that might mislead. If, in one of these books, I stumble across something that seems opposed to the truth, I have no hesitation in saying that my copy is faulty or the translator has not fully grasped what was said, or else I myself have not fully understood.[45]

While the original autographs no longer exist, the faithful and conscientious work of copyists in preserving the words of the original text is miraculous within itself. James Gray, former president of the Moody Bible Institute, says that through the abundance of manuscripts and competent scholarship we have in 999 cases out of every thousand the very word of the original text.

Frederic Kenyon, who spent a lifetime studying biblical manuscripts, writes concerning the preservation of the biblical text, after thousands of manuscripts have been studied and compared, "It is reassuring at the end to find that the general result of all these discoveries and all this study is to strengthen the proof of the authenticity of the Scriptures and our conviction that we have in our hands, in substantial integrity, the veritable word of God."[46]

The same God, who divinely inspired the original author's, as well, has preserved His revelation to humanity through the work of dedicated copyists and scholars. While there are many reliable English translations available today, when speaking of divine inspiration of the Bible, it refers to the original autographs which, through the process of copyists' preservation, have in effect been restored.

What Inspiration Does Mean

Having seen what biblical inspiration is not, what then is meant by the divine inspiration of the Bible? In defining divine inspiration of the Bible Carl Henry writes:

> Inspiration is that supernatural influence of the Holy Spirit whereby the sacred writers were divinely supervised in their production of Scripture, being restrained from error and guided in the choice of words they used, consistently with their disparate personalities and stylistic peculiarities.[47]

In regard to the inspiration of the Bible, James Draper writes, "By inspiration we mean that the Bible is accurate in all that it says and that it will not deceive its readers theologically, historically, chronologically, geographically, or scientifically . . . whatever it says, the Bible says it accurately."[48]

Divine inspiration means that the Lord directed, oversaw and overruled each writer's particular deficiencies, flaws, and imperfections so as to not allow any human error to be imposed or intrude upon His holy Word. Being divinely inspired means the Bible is infallible and without error.

The noted Bible scholar John A. Broadus (1827-1895) says the writers "were preserved by the Holy Spirit from error." While it is not the intent of the Bible to be a book on science or history, yet because it is infallible and without error, it is accurate in what it says in those areas.

Answering the charges of those who contend the Bible teaches scientific errors, Alvah Hovey (1820-1903), one time president of Newton Theological Institution, responds:

> Believers in the truth of Scriptures . . . have no fear of true science, no desire to prevent men from studying the works of God in nature . . . [That it] teaches scientific errors, all references to matters of science in the Bible are (1) Merely incidental and auxiliary; (2) Clothed in popular language [of the day]; and (3) Confirmed by consciousness, so far

as they relate to the mind. Remembering these facts, we say that the Bible has not been shown to contain scientific errors—astronomy, geology, ethnology . . . Bearing in mind these facts, it will be impossible for us to find in the Bible any contradictions which mar its excellence.[49]

Norman Geisler says of inspiration, "[That] the inspiration of the Bible extends to everything it teaches whether spiritual or factual. Inspiration means that whatever the Bible teaches is true, is actually true."[50]

Liberal theologians contend the Bible contains the Word of God, limiting inspiration to some of the teachings of Jesus, the spiritual teachings throughout the Bible and some of the prophetic portions. Who, though, can or is going to decide what is inspired and is the true Word of God and what is not?

Divine inspiration means the whole of the Bible, both the Old Testament and the New Testament, is inspired not just part of it. If that is not the case we have a fallible Bible with errors. The Bible claims itself to be all inspired and God-breathed, not just parts of it (2 Timothy 3:16) and the "Scriptures cannot be broken" (John 10:35). To believe otherwise is to have a Bible that is not trustworthy or reliable. James Draper says, "To suggest that the Bible is in error at any point is to suggest that there is some authority that is more accurate than Scripture and which can be used to correct Scripture."[51]

Not only is the whole of the Bible divinely inspired, infallible and without error, the very words not just the thoughts and concepts, are inspired. The biblical writers did not just summarize the thoughts and concepts of God, but they were verbally inspired, the very words they penned were inspired. When Moses was on Mount Sinai receiving instruction from the Lord, he did not just write down the thoughts and concepts of the Lord, but it reads, "And Moses wrote all the words of the Lord . . ." (Exodus 24:4).

In regard to verbal inspiration James M. Gray (1851-1935) says:

Inspiration includes not only all the books of the Bible, but the words as well . . . This is called the verbal theory of inspiration. If God gave [the writers] only the thought, permitting them to express it in their own words, what guarantee have we that they have done so? It is impossible to know what He says except we have His words.[52]

B.H. Carroll, founder of Southwestern Baptist Theological Seminary (1908), Fort Worth, Texas, eloquently writes concerning verbal inspiration:

It has always been a matter of profound surprise to me that anybody should ever question the verbal inspiration of the Bible. The whole thing had to be written in words. Words are signs of ideas, and if the words are not inspired, then there is no way of getting at anything in connection with inspiration. If I am free to pick up the Bible and read something and say, 'That is inspired,' then read something else and say, 'That is not inspired,' and someone else does not agree with me as to which is and which is not inspired, it leaves the whole thing unsettled as to whether any of it is inspired. What is the object of inspiration? It is to put accurately, in human words, ideas from God. If the words are not inspired, how am I to know how much to reject, and how to find out whether anything is from God? When you hear the silly talk that the Bible 'contains' the Word of God and is not the Word of God, you hear a fool's talk . . . There can be no inspiration of the book without inspiration of the words of the book.[53]

Having seen the Bible's claim to being God's divine revelation to humanity and its claim to being an inspired, God-breathed-out book, what is the Bible's claim to being authoritative?

The Bible's Claim To Being Authoritative

Not only is the Bible God's self-disclosure of Himself to humanity, not only is it divinely inspired, the Bible claims it is authoritative. The authoritative nature of the Bible is seen in the phrases, "God said" and "Thus says the Lord . . . ," which occur over 2,500 times. There are similar expressions that speak of the authoritative nature of the Bible like, "It is written . . ." and "The Word of the Lord came unto me . . ."

Jesus Christ, in whom God's revelation came to culmination, declared after His resurrection and shortly before His ascension, "All authority has been given to Me in heaven and on earth." (Matt 28:18) Even His enemies recognized the authoritative nature of His teaching, confessing, "He taught them as one having authority" (Mark 1:22). Authority rests in the written Word, as well as in the Living Word.

What is meant by the Bible's authoritative nature? Concerning the principle of biblical authority, Christian theologian J.I. Parker comments:

> Its basic principle is that the teaching of the written Scriptures is the word which God spoke and speaks to His Church, and is finally authoritative for faith and life . . . . that is to say, [the Bible] contains all that the Church needs to know in this world for its guidance in the way of salvation and service.[54]

Billy Graham writes, "When we say the Bible is authoritative, we mean that it is God's binding revelation to us. We submit to it because it has come from God. Suppose we ask: What is the source of our religious knowledge? The answer is, the Bible, and it is authoritative for us."[55]

Harold Lindsell says, "By [biblical authority] I mean that we are to believe what it teaches and to practice what it commands. It is the Christian's only rule of faith and life, and all the opinions of men and women are to be tested against it. What contradicts it we need not believe."[56]

Concerning the authority of the Bible, the Westminster Confession (1646), reads:

> The authority of the Holy Scriptures, for which it ought to be believed and obeyed, dependeth not upon the testimony of any man or church, but wholly upon God (who is truth

itself), the author thereof; and therefore it is to be received, because it is the word of God.

In the spiritual arena of faith, the Bible is authoritative in regard to what it says about the plight and predicament of humanity. The Bible is clear that man is not what he was created to be. Disobedience to the Creator brought sin into the world. The plight and predicament of man is that he is a sinner. Paul was clear about man's condition, "All have sinned and come short of the glory of God" (Rom. 3:23). The Bible is authoritative in its summarization of man that he is "dead in trespasses and sins" (Ephesians 2:1). Our sins have separated us from the very God who created us and desires to fellowship with us (Genesis 3:7-8).

No amount of reforming, turning over a new leaf, good works, or resolutions can change the fact that at man's core he is a sinner who has missed the mark of what God would have him to be and that by our own efforts that fellowship with God cannot be restored. The Bible is clear and authoritative regarding this matter. What is man to do then?

The Good News of God's revelation to humanity is that even in spite of man's predicament; God has Himself offered and given a provision for our plight. Humanities provision is found in the person of Jesus Christ. The Bible is authoritative in its declaration that Christ is man's only provision for the problem of sin and broken fellowship. The Bible, the record of the revelation of God which culminated in Jesus Christ, authoritatively declares to humanity that though all have sinned all who come to Christ can be forgiven "freely by his grace through the redemption that is in Christ Jesus" (Romans 3:24).

Jesus declared on the authority that was vested in Him by God, the spiritual thirst that plagues humanity can be quenched, "If any man thirst let him come to [Christ] and drink. He that believes in [Christ] as the scripture has said, out of his heart will flow rivers of living water" (John 7:37-38).

The provision that humanity needs, in order for restoration of fellowship with God and, our sins, which broke that fellowship to be removed, is found in Jesus Christ. Try as man may he cannot remove his sins or restore that lost fellowship in his own efforts. Peter authoritatively proclaimed that that can only be accomplished when one turns to the crucified Christ whom God raised from the dead; for "nor is there salvation in any other, there is no other name under heaven given among men, by which we must be saved" (Acts 4:8-12). On the authority of the Scripture, those who embrace God's provision for man's plight, as found in Jesus Christ, discovers that, "whosoever shall call upon the name of the Lord [Jesus Christ] shall be saved" (Romans 10:13).

The Bible is authoritative in regard to stating man's plight and predicament, authoritative in its proclaiming Christ as man's provision, and is also authoritative in matters of doctrinal, moral, ethical, and practical living. The Creator, who created man, has not left him wandering in a moral maze, pondering some existential philosophy as to the best way to conduct oneself and live on this earth.

In the Bible, the revelation of God to man, one finds not only how forgiveness and restored fellowship with God is possible, but within its pages, one finds a spiritual manual for faith and practice and everyday living. Claiming itself divinely inspired, the Bible claims that it is also sufficient and "profitable for doctrine, for reproof, for correction, for instruction in righteousness . . ." (II Tim 3:16).

J.I. Packer writes, "Those who acknowledge the Lordship of Christ are bound to accept the principle of biblical authority [in their lives]."[57] This truth is evident throughout the Bible.

When God gave Moses the Ten Commandments, He was revealing to Israel that He was not only a redemptive God, but a holy God of moral standards (Exodus 20). They were given as authoritative commandments of how Israel should conduct their lives individually and collectively.

When the writer(s) of Proverbs penned their pithy words of advice, they were expressions of how God wanted His people to morally and ethically conduct themselves in the way that was in the best interest of the individual and society as a whole.

When Jesus preached the Sermon on the Mount, He revealed that while He was not only a Savior who came to redeem, but was also a Savior who came to reveal how Kingdom citizens are to conduct themselves in public and in private. When the Apostles, through the inspiration of the Holy Spirit, penned the Epistles, they not only were expounding upon the redemptive work of Christ and correct doctrine, but also encouraged and exhorted the readers to live a life that exemplified the Redeemer, Jesus Christ.

To those who accept the truthfulness of the Bible in regard to its revelation and inspiration, it is only normative that it be accepted as authoritative in matters of doctrine, faith and practice, and in matters of moral, ethical, and practical living. Humanity has not been left to construct its own system of morality, which is the reason the world is in chaos today, but in His revealed, inspired, authoritative Word, the Bible, He has given us moral and ethical principles by which to live.

It is clear what the Bible claims about itself. It claims to be the revealed, divinely inspired, authoritative Word of God and it beckons humanity to heed its message as it is found in the written word, the Bible, and the Living Word, Jesus Christ.

The question arises: Does the lofty view the Bible proclaims for itself, have support in history and are there any witnesses that can attest to the Bible's claims? It behooves us to call to the witness stand from history, witnesses to discover the answer to that question.

CHAPTER 3
CAN WE GET A WITNESS?

The purpose of the last chapter was to discover what the Bible declares about itself. It was established that the Bible claims itself to be God's revelation to humankind, to be divinely inspired, and to be authoritative for faith and living. There was an examination of what each of those terms means and entails.

While appealing to its own testimony of being God's revelation, inspired, and His authoritative Word, are there witnesses that can be summoned into the court of truth from the arena of history to verify the Bible's claims? It will be the purpose of this chapter to listen to the voices of witnesses from throughout history whose testimony will corroborate the Bible's declaration and claims.

Witnesses From Persons Within The Bible

The first witnesses worthy of attention, in regard to the Bible being divinely inspired, are from the testimony of personages that are found within the pages of the Bible. Their voices will give insight into their understanding of how the Bible is to be viewed.

Witness of the Prophets

Beginning with the prophets of the Old Testament, they with deep convictions, affirmed the words they spoke and wrote came from the Lord.

The writer of Hebrews informs that God "spoke in time past to the fathers by the prophets" (Heb. 1:1). Peter writes, "Knowing this first, that no prophecy of the Scripture is of any private interpretation, for prophecy never came by the will of man, but holy men of God spoke as they were moved by the Holy Spirit" (2 Peter 1:20-21).

These two verses tell us the messages and writings of the prophets were not from their own volition, but were given to them directly from the Lord. The witness and testimony of the prophets unquestionably agree with this truth.

When Moses was called by the Lord to deliver the children of Israel from bondage, he told the Lord he could not speak well. The Lord informed Moses telling him, "Now therefore go, and I will be with your mouth, and teach you what you shall say" (Exodus 4:12). The words Moses was to speak were not his own but came directly from the Lord.

Further in Exodus it reads, "And the Lord said unto Moses, 'Write thou these words: for after the tenor of these words I have made a covenant with thee and with Israel'" (Ex. 34:27). The words Moses penned in this incident were not his own but the words of the Lord.

In Numbers, the Lord declares Moses to be a prophet with whom He had direct communication. The Word informs that Moses was given more than just the thoughts or concepts of what the Lord wanted him to say and write, but says of His communication with Moses, "I will speak with him face to face, even plainly, and not in dark sayings . . ." (Num. 12:1-8).

When the Lord was giving Moses instructions to give the Israelites, He told Moses he was to speak and record the very Words of God and not deviate any. The passage reads, "You shall not add to the word which I command you, nor take from it, that ye may keep the commandments of the Lord your God which I command you" (Deut. 4:2).

There are many more passages that could be looked at that give testimony that what Moses wrote and spoke were the inspired authoritative words from the Lord.

As Jeremiah began his prophetic ministry one reads, "But the Lord said unto me, Do not say, 'I am a youth.' For you shall go to all to whom I send you, and whatever I command you, you shall speak. Do not be afraid of their faces; for I am with you to deliver you, says the Lord. Then the Lord put forth His hand and touched my mouth. And the Lord said unto me, 'Behold, I have put my words in your mouth'" (Jeremiah 1:7-9).

Over and over we find Jeremiah writing that the words he spoke and recorded were not his, but "the word of the Lord came to me saying . . ." (Jeremiah 2:1; 7:1; 11:1; 16:1; 18:1; 21:1; 30:1; 32:1; 34:1; 40:1; 46:1). Jeremiah was to speak and record the very words of the Lord, not his own.

Jeremiah records, "And it came to pass, that when Jeremiah had made an end of speaking unto all the people all the words of the Lord their God, for which the Lord their God had sent him to them even all these words" (Jer. 43:1). Like the sin of Judah, what Jeremiah wrote was "with a pen of iron and with the point of a diamond . . ." (Jeremiah 17:1).

All through Jeremiah it is abundantly clear his words were not his but "the word of the Lord." Throughout the writings of Jeremiah one will find almost one hundred times phrases that declare that his writings and words were not his but inspired by the Lord.

Isaiah, the poetic prophet, declared that what he wrote and spoke were not his words but the very words of the Lord. As Isaiah began his ministry, he let it be known that the people were to, "Hear the word of the Lord . . ." (Isaiah 1:10) Throughout Isaiah one finds no fewer than twenty times does he clearly declare that his writings are the "words of the Lord."

Ezekiel gives testimony that his words and messages were divinely inspired. Ezekiel writes, "Moreover [the Lord] said unto me, 'Son of man, receive into your heart all my words that I shall speak to you, and hear with your ears. And go, get to the captives, to the children of your people, and speak unto them, and tell them, Thus says the Lord God . . .'" (Ezekiel 3:10-11).

Ezekiel expressed to the people that his words were not his own but inspired words from the Spirit of the Lord. Ezekiel says of being inspired by the Spirit, "Then Spirit of the Lord fell upon me, and said unto me, 'Speak! Thus says the Lord . . .'" (Ezekiel 11:5).

Micah, who predicted that Jesus would be born in Bethlehem (5:2), writes from where he got his words, "The word of the Lord that came to Micah . . ." (1:1). He declares that his message came directly from the Lord (3:2), and he delivered those messages "full of power by the Spirit of the Lord" (3:8). He encouraged the people to "hear now what the Lord says" (6:1), and hear "the Lord's voice" (6:9).

Daniel was continually hearing "the voice of His words" (Daniel 10:9), which "he wrote" down and recorded (Daniel 7:1-2; 8:1; 10:1). History has shown Daniel's predications to be accurate, information he could not have known unless it was by divine inspiration given to him.

Daniel, whose predications of future world empires came to pass, always gave the Lord the glory for messages he received. When Daniel was asked to interpret the dream of Nebuchadnezzar, he went before the Lord for the answer. He writes, "Then was the secret revealed to Daniel in a night vision. So Daniel blessed the God of heaven" (Daniel 2:19). The interpretations Daniel received were obviously not his but inspired by the Lord.

These are only a few of the numerous verses and prophets that could be examined in which the prophet gives testimony and confirms the truth that their words and writings were divinely inspired. Other prophets could give the same witness as to their unique communication with and from the Lord (Hosea 1:1; Joel 1:1; Amos 3:1; Obadiah 1:1; Jonah 1:1; Nahum 1:12; Habakkuk 2:2; Haggai 1:1; Malachi 1:1). They all give testimony to the fact that their words and writings were inspired by the Lord.

Witness of Jesus

The most significant witness who attests to the revelation, inspiration and authority of the Scriptures is Jesus Christ, the Son of God. Unmatched in His words, His teachings, His life, and His many astounding works; it behooves one to listen to His assessment and testimony regarding the Scriptures. In doing so one will discover that Jesus esteemed the Old Testament text in the highest possible position and within its pages He declared one could hear the very voice of God.

Jesus regarded the Old Testament as the inspired Word of God saying that "scripture cannot be broken" (John 10:35). He held Scripture to be authoritative as seen in His Temptations in the Wilderness. When confronted with the Devil, Jesus responded by saying, "It is written,

'Man shall not live by bread alone, but by every word that proceeds out of the mouth of God'" (Matt. 4:4). Jesus was quoting from Deuteronomy 8:3 which He affirmed came from "the mouth of God." In His confrontation with the devil in the wilderness he found refuge three times in "it is written."

Jesus declares the Old Testament to be truth as He requests of the Father on behalf of the disciples, "Sanctify them by Your truth: Your word is truth" (John 17:17).

Jesus regarded the whole of the Old Testament to be inspired, not just part of it. In the Sermon on the Mount Jesus spoke concerning the totality of Scripture being inspired when he said, "Do not think that I came to destroy the Law or the prophets. I did not come to destroy, but to fulfill. For assuredly, I say unto you, till heaven and earth pass away, one jot or tittle will by no means pass from the law, till all is fulfilled" (Matthew 5:17-18).

Jesus is explicitly clear that not one jot, which was the smallest letter in the Hebrew alphabet, or one tittle, which was a small point in the Hebrew letters, was to be removed from Scripture. He was saying that the smallest or least part of the Scripture is not to be destroyed or altered.

Jesus confirms that the Old Testament was the revelation of God's redemptive purpose of how He worked though people, events and history for the express purpose of bringing a Savior into the world, of which He was the fulfillment. Jesus said, "You search the Scriptures, for in them think you have eternal life; and these [are] they which testify of me" (John 5:39).

On the evening of the first day of His resurrection, He walked with two travelers on the road to Emmaus and expounded unto them the unfolding of God's redemptive purpose. He said unto them, "O foolish ones, and slow of heart to believe in all that the prophets have spoken! Ought not Christ to have suffered these things, and to enter into His glory? And beginning at Moses and all the Prophets, He expounded unto them in all the Scriptures the things concerning Himself." (Luke 24:25-27). In these two incidents Jesus was attesting to the inspired revelation of the whole of Scripture as God's redemptive purpose which found fulfillment in Christ.

Jesus equated knowing the Scriptures with, as well, knowing the power of God in one's life. He rebuked the Sadducees and "said unto them, 'You are mistaken, not knowing the scriptures, nor the power of God'" (Matt. 22:29).

While teaching in the temple, when referring to Psalm 110, a Psalm of David, Jesus taught that the words David penned were not his, but were inspired by the Spirit of the Lord. He says that "for David himself said by the Holy Spirit . . . ." (Mark 12:36).

Jesus, on numerous occasions, confirmed the authority of Scripture by using the phrase, "It is written." (Matthew 4:4, 7, 10; 26:24; Luke 18:31-33; 22:37).

Jesus in affirming the Old Testament as God's inspired, authoritative revelation, also expressed his belief in the history of the events and persons of the Old Testament. Jesus did not view the events and persons of the Old Testament as fables, folklore, or myths, but as actual events and people. He taught as historical Adam and Eve (Matthew 19:4), the flood of Noah (Luke 17:27), Jonah and the whale (Matthew 12:40), the miracles of Elijah (Luke 4:25), Moses lifting up the serpent in the wilderness (John 3:14), the manna that fell from heaven (John 6:32), Sodom and Gomorrah's destruction (Luke 17:29), and the reality of Abraham and Jacob (Matthew 22:32).

While many Higher Critics dispute Moses being the author of the first five books of the Old Testament, Jesus held to the authorship of Moses. In regard to Moses being the author of the Pentateuch, Jesus verified His authorship when He said, "Moses wrote . . ." (Mark 10:5; 12:19; John 5:46).

Jesus not only testified to the inspiration of the Old Testament, He laid the foundation for the inspiration of the New Testament which was soon to be written. He saw the coming record of the New Testament as fulfilling of the Old Testament which did "testify" of Him (John 5:39). His very words and work were to be the bedrock on which the New Testament would be constructed. Jesus declared, "Heaven and earth will pass away, but My words will by no means pass away" (Luke 21:33).

We find Jesus in declaring the words He spoke were not mere human words but authoritative and divinely inspired by the Spirit, "The words that I speak to you are spirit, they are life" (John 6:63). Peter recognized the inspiration of Jesus' words confessing they were "the words of eternal life" (John 6:68). Jesus told his disciples on the night of His arrest that the Holy Spirit would guide them into "all truth" (John 16:13), and "teach them all things" (John 14:26), giving hint and anticipation of the New Testament which was yet to be written.

The words of Jesus being spirit, life, and eternal, are authoritative for faith and living, and He issues a universal call, "Therefore whoever hears these sayings of Mine, and does them, I will liken him to a wise man who built his house on the rock" (Matthew 7:24).

Jesus, without question, affirmed the authenticity of the Old Testament and had an unshakeable conviction that it was God's divinely inspired, authoritative revelation to humankind. Norman Geisler writes, "On the testimony and authority of Christ it is established as true that the Old Testament, with all of its historical and miraculous events, is an inscripturated revelation of God."[58]

Herbert Lockyer concludes, "Whenever Jesus referred to Old Testament Scriptures, he invariably did so in terms calculated to inspire the most absolute confidence in all they contained."[59] (Note: For those who desires a detailed examination and scholarly treatment of how Jesus viewed and used the Old Testament, refer to *Jesus and the Old Testament* by R.T. France.)

Witness of the Apostles

The witness and testimony of the prophets and Jesus has been examined in regard to their attesting to the inspiration of the Old Testament. How did the Apostles regard the Old Testament and their own writings and those of other Apostles?

Paul viewed the Old Testament as divinely inspired and God-breathed. He declares, "All scripture is given by inspiration of God"(2 Tim. 3:16). As has been pointed out earlier, B.H. Carroll says the word "inspiration" literally means, "God-breathed-out."[60] Paul, using the word "all," implies that he believed the whole of the Old Testament was inspired not just part of it. Paul affirmed the importance and authority of the Old Testament when he wrote, "For whatever things were written before were written for our learning, that we through patience and comfort of the Scriptures might have hope" (Romans 15:4).

After careful reading of the last chapter of the Epistle of Romans, one will see Paul gives equal rank to both the Old Testament Scriptures and the current writings that were being written by the Apostles that are a "revelation of the mystery" of Jesus Christ (Romans 16:25-26). In Ephesians, Paul speaks of his writings as being "by revelation" (Eph. 3:3-4).

In writing to the Corinthians, he was cognizant that what he was writing was, "not I, but the Lord" (I Corinthians 7:10). He tells the Corinthians, "These things we also speak, not in the words which man's wisdom teaches, but which the Holy Spirit teaches, comparing spiritual things with spiritual" (I Corinthians 2:13). Paul affirms that what he was writing was not human wisdom but wisdom from the Lord.

Paul expresses gratitude to the Christians at Thessalonica for receiving the word that was delivered unto them as the inspired Word of God. Paul writes, "For this reason we also thank God without ceasing, because, when ye received the word of God which you heard from us, you welcomed it not as the word of men, but as it is in truth, the word of God, which also effectively works in you who believe"(I Thessalonians 2:13).

It is rather evident that Paul held to the inspiration of the Old Testament, and, as well, contended that his apostolic writings, which would eventually comprise the New Testament, also were inspired.

Like Paul, Peter embraced the divine inspiration of the Old Testament writing, "For prophecy never came by the will of man, but holy men of God spoke as they were moved by the Holy Spirit" (2 Peter 1:21). Peter attests that what the writers of the Old Testament wrote, they did so under the influence of "the Spirit of Christ who was in them was indicating when He testified beforehand the sufferings of Christ . . ." (I Peter 1:11). Peter confirms that when David wrote in the Psalms it was "the Holy Spirit by the mouth of David" speaking (Acts 1:16).

Peter, also like Paul, equated the Old Testament and Apostolic writings as equally inspired. He writes, "That you may be mindful of the words which were spoken before by the holy prophets and of the commandment of us, the apostles of the Lord and Savior" (2 Peter 3:2).

Peter contended that Paul's writings were just as inspired as was the Old Testament. Peter writes, "And consider that the longsuffering of our Lord is salvation—as also our beloved brother Paul, according to the wisdom given unto him has written to you, as also in all his epistles, speaking in them of these things; in which are some things hard to understand, which untaught and unstable people twist to their own destruction, as they do also the rest of the Scriptures" (2 Peter 3:15-16).

Commenting on these verses Nathaniel West (1794-1864) writes:

> The Apostle Peter tells us that he was in possession, not merely of some of Paul's Epistles, but "all his Epistles," and places them canonically in the same rank with what he calls "the other Scriptures." i.e., of equal inspiration and authority with the "words spoken before by the Holy Prophets, and the commandment of the Lord and Savior, through the Apostles" (2 Peter 3:2, 16).[61]

Both Paul and Peter testify to the inspiration and authority of the Old Testament, as well as verifying the inspiration of the New Testament which was in the process of being written and compiled.

The author of Hebrew also affirms the inspiration of the Old Testament when he writes, "God, who at various times and in various ways spoke in time past to the fathers by the prophets, has in these last days spoken unto us by His Son, whom He has appointed heir of all things, through whom also He made the worlds" (Hebrews 1:1-2). The author of Hebrews, as well, in chapter eleven, attests to the historical reality of Old Testament personages of Abel, Noah, Abraham, Jacob, Joseph, Moses, Joshua and Jericho, Rahab, Gideon, Samson and the judges, David, Samuel, and the prophets.

Other New Testament writers also affirm the inspiration and authoritativeness of the Old Testament. James speaks of the miracles of Elijah as factual (James 5:17-20); Mark began his Gospel quoting from Malachi 3:1 and in doing so appeals to the authority of the Old Testament (Mark 1:2); Luke builds his Gospel not only on "eyewitnesses" accounts of the life of Jesus, but also builds his case for Christ on appealing to the Old Testament writings which he deems authoritative (Luke 2:23–24; 3:4–6); John cites from the Old Testament prophets that gives his Gospel more authoritative weight before the readers (2:17; 12:14–15, 38, 40; 19:24, 36, 37), and Jude, in his short epistle, speaks of being historically true Sodom and Gomorrah, Moses, Balaam, and Enoch.

Without question, the New Testament writers give testimony to and affirm the truthfulness and reliability of the Old Testament. They understood and had full confidence that the Old Testament was the inspired, authoritative revelation of God to humankind. The New Testament writers not only attested to the inspiration of the Old Testament, but the early writings of the Apostles were also embraced as inspired.

Harold Lindsell remarks:

> No one can read any part of the New Testament without being impressed by the fact that the writers convey the sense of divine authority, manifest the badge of truthfulness, and give no impression whatever that what they wrote, or what [the prophets wrote] or the other apostles wrote, should or could be doubted by the reader.[62]

The Apostle John, as he comes to the close of the last book in the Bible, Revelation, ends with fitting words which sum up the book but also fitting words to sum up the whole of the Bible, both Old and New Testament: "And [the Lord] said to me, 'These words are faithful and true: and the Lord God of the holy prophets . . .'" (Revelation 22:6, KJV).

Witness of the Holy Spirit

The fourth witness from within the Bible that affirms its inspiration is the Holy Spirit. The Holy Spirit was the agent or instrumentality through which God communicated His divine truth to the biblical writers. The writers wrote as "they were moved by the Holy Spirit" (2 Peter 1:21).

Jesus twice affirmed the Holy Spirit is the, "The Spirit of truth" (John 14:17; 16:13); therefore, the Holy Spirit's communication to the biblical writers could not contain anything of error but only truth. Not only was the Holy Spirit the one who was the instrumentality who inspired the writers to pen truth, the Holy Spirit is the one who will guide into understanding the truth of what has been written (John 14:26; 16:13).

The Holy Spirit does not draw attention to Himself but to point humanity to the One whom the redemptive purpose of the Bible speaks, Jesus Christ. Jesus said the Holy Spirit "shall not speak of himself" (John 16:13), but "shall glorify me" (John 16:14).

Commenting on the witness of the Holy Spirit in the inspiration of the Bible, John Calvin writes in his masterful work, *Institutes of the Christian Religion,* "The testimony of the Holy Spirit is superior to all reason . . . It is necessary therefore, that the same Spirit who spoke by the mouths of the prophets, should penetrate into our hearts, to convince us that they faithfully delivered the oracles which were divinely entrusted to them."[63]

It is the Holy Spirit who "bears witness with our spirit" (Romans 8:16) of the authenticity and integrity of the Bible. The Holy Spirit only bears witness in agreement and in harmony with the written Word of God. The truth as to the inspiration of the whole of Scripture, John Calvin contends, "obtains the credit which it deserves with us by the testimony of the Spirit."

The voices from four witnesses from within the Bible have been heard from as to their testimony regarding the truthfulness and inspiration of the Bible: the prophets, Jesus, the apostles, and the Holy Spirit. All four attest to and confidently affirm the Bible is unequivocally the inspired and authoritative revelation of God.

Witnesses From History

As one journeys back through history, are there witnesses that can be called into the court of truth who can give affirming testimony to the Bible's inspiration? While the witness list is endless, some representative voices will be considered that will give a historical perspective of how the Bible has been viewed in regard to the genuineness of its inspiration.

Jewish Historian Josephus

One of the earliest voices after the death, burial and resurrection of Christ, who wrote about the inspiration of Scripture was Josephus (ca. 37-100), a first century Jewish historian. He is best known for his extensive work on Jewish history entitled, *Antiquities of the Jews.* Josephus writes of the books of the Jewish Old Testament:

> [They] which are justly accredited as divine . . . . For although so many ages have passed away; no one has dared to add to them, or to take anything from, or to make alterations. In all Jews it is implanted, even from their birth, to regard them as being the instructions of God, and to abide steadfastly by them, and if necessary, to die for them.[64]

Sprinkled throughout the writings of Josephus one can find such statements regarding the Old Testament as, "There is no discrepancy in the facts recorded . . . [as the prophets] . . . by reason of the inspiration they received from God."[65] He attested to the historical reality of Isaiah and the prophets, and that Moses wrote the first five books of the Bible. One who reads Josephus soon realizes he held a supremely high view of the Old Testament, affirming it, along with the Jews of his day, to be divinely inspired.

Early Church Fathers

When one examines the writings of the early Church Fathers their embracing and affirming the divine inspiration of the Bible is most evident. (For quotes from the Early Church Fathers see, *The Ante-Nicene Fathers*, New York: Scribner's, 1899.)

Polycarp (ca. 69-155), who was a disciple of the Apostle John, spoke of the Bible as being "the oracles of the Lord." Irenaeus (died 202), who writes that he heard Polycarp speak as a lad, echoes the words that speak of the Bible's inspiration, writing, "The Scriptures are perfect, inasmuch as they were uttered by the word of God and His Spirit . . . The writers spoke as acted on by the Spirit . . . The writers are beyond all falsehood."

Clement of Rome, who died in 102, urges one to "look carefully into the Scriptures which are the true utterances of the Holy Spirit." Justin Martyr (ca. 105-165) says that "the history which Moses wrote by divine inspiration, the Holy Spirit taught."

Clement of Alexandria (ca. 150-211) says the Bible is a firm foundation, writing, "The foundations of our faith rest on no insecure basis. We have received them through God Himself . . . for the mouth of the Lord, the Holy Spirit, spoke it."

Origen (185-253), one of the leading scholars and theologians of the early church, emphatically writes in affirming the inspiration of the Bible:

> It is the doctrine acknowledged by all Christians and evidently preached in the churches, that the Holy Spirit inspired the saints, prophets and apostles, and was present in those of old time, as in those He inspired at the coming of Christ; for Christ, the Word of God, was in Moses when he wrote, and in the prophets, and by His Spirit He did speak to them all things. The records of the Gospels are the Oracles of the Lord, pure Oracles purified as silver seven times tried. They are without error, since they were accurately written by the co-operation of the Holy Spirit.[66]

Gregory of Wyssa (ca. 335-394), who sought to defend the Christianity against Greek philosophy, wrote that when one reads the Bible one is to recognize, "Whatsoever the divine Scripture says is the voice of the Holy Spirit."

From Augustine And Beyond

Augustine (354-430), whose influence spanned the fourth and fifth centuries, is considered by many scholars to be one of the greatest theologians the Christian faith has ever produced. He held the Bible in high esteem as evidenced by stating, "The Scriptures are the letters of God, the voice of God, the writings of God." Commenting on the Four Gospels he writes," We must demonstrate that the four sacred writers are not at variance . . . . I have learned to ascribe to those books which are of canonical rank, and only them, such reverence and honor, that I firmly believe that no single error due to the author is found in any one of them . . . . Therefore, we yield to and agree to the authority of the Holy Scripture which can neither be deceived nor deceive."[67]

Jerome (342-420), who translated the Bible into Latin (Vulgate), attested to the inspiration of the Bible calling them "divine Scriptures" and they being "the bonds of truth."

When one listens to the voices of those of the powerful Reformation Movement it is discovered they built the reforming movement on the foundation that the Bible was the inspired Word of God. Martin Luther (1483-1546), the Father of the Reformation, stated of the Bible, "This is our foundation where the Holy Scripture establishes something that must be believed, there we must not deviate from the words as they sound, neither from the order as it stands . . . The Scriptures have never erred . . . For whoever despises a single word of God does not regard any as important."[68]

John Calvin (1509-1564), a second generation Reformer, was more than clear in his affirmation regarding inspiration of the Bible. He taught that one ought to approach the Bible with . . . .

> . . . . the same reverence which we owe to God . . . We ought to embrace with mild docility, and without exception, whatever is delivered in the Holy Scriptures. For Scripture is the school of the Holy Spirit in which as nothing useful and necessary is omitted, so nothing is taught which is not profitable to know . . . . The divine origin of Scripture, the fact that it has come 'from heaven' is that to which the Spirit gives witness, and this transfers authority from men to God.[69]

Throughout his writings Calvin attested to the Bible being "the pure word of God," "the sure and infallible record," "the infallible rule of His holy truth," "free from every stain or defect," and "the certain and unerring rule."

John Smyth (1570-1612), who most historians contend, organized the first Baptist church in Amsterdam in 1609, affirmed the divine inspiration of the Bible, writing, "Men are of two sorts, inspired or ordinary men. Men inspired by the Holy Ghost are the Holy Prophets and Apostles who wrote the Holy Scriptures by inspiration." Thomas Helwys (1575-c. 1616), close companion of Smyth, wrote in 1611, that the Old and New Testament were inspired, "and therefore to be used with all reverence as containing the Holy Word of God, which only is our direction in all things whatsoever." [70]

Considered the Father of Religious Freedom, Roger Williams (1603-1684), who established the first Baptist church in America, in 1638, Providence, Rhode Island, taught "of what Christ said and did and of all the rest of the Scripture" to be inspired and authoritative. This view of the Bible was prevalent among Baptists in America, as the Philadelphia Association stated in 1742, "We believe the Holy Bible was written by men divinely inspired . . . that it has God for its author, salvation for its end, and truth, without any mixture of error, for its matter . . ." [71]

One of the greatest and most influential preachers ever on American soil, who was a key leader in the Great Awakening that swept through the colonies, was Jonathan Edwards (1703-1758). He said, "The Scriptures are evidence of their own divine authority . . . ." He unquestionably believed the Scriptures are the word and work of a divine mind.

Charles Haddon Spurgeon (1834-1892), the silver-tongued English preacher labeled the prince of preachers, regarding the inspiration of the Bible, poetically wrote in 1855:

> Since God wrote it, mark its truthfulness . . . . this is the Word of God. Come, search, ye critics, and find a flaw; examine it from its Genesis to its Revelation and find an error. This is a vein of pure gold, unalloyed by quartz or any earthy substance. This is a star without a speck; a sun without a blot; a light without darkness; a moon without paleness; a glory without dimness. O Bible! It cannot be said of any other book, that it is perfect and pure; but of thee we can declare all wisdom is gathered up in thee,

without a particle of folly . . . . This is the book untainted by any error, but is pure, unalloyed, perfect truth. Why? Because God wrote it . . . . Blessed Bible, thou art all truth.[72]

Spurgeon was truly a champion of the Bible and affirming its inspiration was a passion that sent him to the front line to defend it when the winds of Higher Criticism began blowing in England.

Augustus H. Strong (1836-1921), whose theological influence spanned the last half of the nineteenth and the first half of the twentieth century, said that inspiration of the Bible was "supernatural, plenary, and dynamical." The Bible was "divine revelation, sufficient, when taken together and interpreted by the same Spirit who inspired them, to lead every honest inquirer to Christ and to salvation."[73]

Evangelist and writer John R. Rice (1895-1980), who was a key leader in Christian Fundamentalism, wrote regarding inspiration, "It is the only absolutely reliable Book ever written, because it is the very word of God. It is correct in history and accurate [in all areas]. It is morally perfect . . . the Bible is the infallible Word of God. It is supernatural, perfect, eternal."[74]

British-born J.I. Packer (1926-), much respected Christian thinker and writer, attests to the Bible's inspiration. He writes:

Scripture is termed infallible and inerrant to express the conviction that all its teaching is the utterance of God 'who cannot lie,' whose word, once spoken, abides forever, and that therefore, it may be trusted implicitly . . . [The] infallibility of Scripture is simply the infallibility of God speaking . . . Its text is word for word God-given; its message is an organic unity, the infallible Word of an infallible God, a web of revealed truths centered upon Christ . . . and its meaning can be grasped only by those who humbly seek and gladly receive the help of the Holy Spirit . . . [The] Bible asks to be regarded as a God-given, error-free, self interpreting unity, true and trustworthy in all that it teaches.[75]

Witnesses from history have affirmed and have given testimony to the Bible being divinely inspired. Beginning with the early Church Fathers and concluding with J.I. Packer, the representative voices examined regarding biblical inspiration can be heard echoing down through the corridors of history. Many more could be called to give testimony in the court of truth in attesting to the divine inspiration of the Bible. There are countless others who beg to be heard: Tertullian, Zwingli, George Whitfield, John Wesley, Charles Hodge, Robert Wilson, John L. Dagg, Dwight L. Moody, R.A. Torrey, B.H. Carroll, W.T. Conner, Benjamin Warfield, Auther W. Pink, A.W. Tozer, W.A. Criswell, J.R. Graves, Donald Guthrie, Norman Giesler, Carl H. Henry, and John R. Stott. All would love to give testimony to the Bible's divinely inspired nature.

Numerous confessions of faith could be examined which attest to and affirm the inspiration of Scripture, such as: the 529 confession of faith called The Canons of the Council of Orange, The Augsburg Confession (1530), The Geneva Confession (1536), The Scots Confession (1560), The Westminster Confession (1647), Second London Baptist Confession (1689), and the Puritan Confession of faith of Charles Spurgeon of 1855. The list is endless, but they all would affirm in their wording, in some form, that the Bible is the inspired, infallible word of God and is to be the sole rule for faith and practice.

No matter how many witnesses are called upon to speak on behalf of biblical inspiration, every voice can be heard beckoning in unison to humanity to come and stand upon the only solid foundation that will give firm footing in a world of sinking sand.

PART II
TRUTHS AFFIRMING THE BIBLE'S DIVINE INSPIRATION

"All Scripture is given by inspiration of God . . ."

II Timothy 3:16

CHAPTER 4
THEMATIC UNITY AFFIRMS BIBLE'S INSPIRATION

Much time has been spent in the previous three chapters laying a foundation regarding varying views concerning the revelation, inspiration, and authority of the Bible. Skeptics and liberal theologians may either challenge such notions or dismiss them altogether, while conservative theologians, by careful examination of the facts, seek to present evidence that affirms the Bible as the divinely inspired Word of God.

There are those who would suggest that all that has been written thus far, that in the end one's viewpoint regarding the Bible is a personal opinion of the individual. Those who pitch their tent in such a camp contend that there are no objective, rational evidences or arguments that support the Bible as being divinely inspired. To the honest inquirer, are there any compelling arguments that verify the truthfulness of the Bible as being divinely inspired? The purpose of this book contends that there are objective and rational truths that support the Bible's divine inspiration.

The first compelling truth that affirms the Bible is divinely inspired is found in its thematic unity, its unity in themes. There is a thread of unity in the major themes of the Bible that tie and bind together all sixty-six books. An examining of this phenomenon reveals a divine Mind behind the Bible.

The Bible one holds in their hands consists of sixty-six books, thirty-nine in the Old Testament and twenty-seven in the New Testament.

Written over a period of about 1,600 years by approximately forty different authors, few stop to consider the uniqueness of the Book of books. From the time Moses penned the first five books of the Bible around 1,450 B.C. until John put the finishing touches on the book of Revelation near the end of the first century A.D., over a millennium and a half had transpired.

Over that period of time, those who were chosen to faithfully record heaven's message to humanity came from a myriad of social, economic, cultural, and educational backgrounds. Moses, who was raised in the palace of Pharaoh, later is found tending sheep on the backside of the desert, authored the Pentateuch (Exodus 1-3). A herdsman from Tekoa, named Amos, penned a book that bears his name (Amos 1:1). Isaiah writes with a poetic beauty that lifts one to the heavens, while the writings of Peter bear the marks of one who made their living as a fisherman who had little formal education. A cup bearer for the Persian king writes Nehemiah, while one who bailed out of a missionary journey with Paul because times got a little tough wrote the Gospel of Mark. A skilled scribe in the Law of Moses penned Ezra, while a Gentile physician authored Luke and Acts. Paul, who wrote almost half of the New Testament, was a man of immense religious, cultural, and educational background, while the writer of many of the Psalms, who later became king of Israel, came from a background of a shepherd boy tending to his father's sheep. Matthew had been a dishonest and disrespected tax collector for the Roman Empire, yet a Gospel bears his name. Solomon was a wealthy king whose wisdom found him penning Ecclesiastes, Song of Solomon, and many of the Proverbs. A man whose once fiery disposition wanted to call fire down from heaven to destroy those who disagreed with Christ, wrote the Gospel of John, I, 2, and 3 John, and Revelation, while a man with a broken heart over the sins of the Jews who became known as the weeping prophet, wrote Jeremiah.

One can clearly see the authors of the Bible vast differences in not only the time frame in which some of the writers lived, some being separated by hundreds of years, but their temperaments, educational, economic and cultural backgrounds varied as well. Though there are obvious differences among the writers of the Bible there is a remarkable feature about what each wrote that cannot be explained by suggesting mere human wisdom as the answer. There is a unity that is interwoven throughout all their writings that bind the sixty-six books, like the cloak of Jesus, into a seamless strand.

Augustus H. Strong writes, "In spite of its variety of authorship and the vast separation of its writers from one another in point of time, there is a unity of subject, spirit, and aim throughout the whole."[76]

The fact of this unity is certainly more than luck or fate. The chances are astronomical that you could pick forty writers over a period of some 1,600 years with extensively different backgrounds, some who never saw the writings of the other, ask them to write on a topic of their choice, and then bring the writings of those forty authors together and there be complete unity in what they wrote! Yet such a unity is the case with the Bible. The Bible's remarkable unity and themes that run through it is a compelling argument for the divine inspiration of the Bible.

Four facets of the jewel of biblical unity will be considered revealing a remarkable unity that is more than mere coincidence.

Monotheistic Unity

First, there is a monotheistic (belief in only one God) unity that runs through the whole of Scripture that reveals biblical harmony. From Genesis to Revelation the Bible does not vary in its monotheistic premise that there is only one true God. "The Lord our God is one God" (Deuteronomy 6:4), is a thread that binds the whole of the Bible.

The biblical writers lived in a culture of tribal polytheism (belief in multiple gods or deities) where people worshipped different gods, and what god or gods one worshipped today may change tomorrow. That there were a people like the Jews who worshipped only one God and not multiple gods was not the rule but the exception. When man is left only with the general revelation of nature he begins to create his own god or gods. (Romans 1:21-23). It is only by special revelation, divine revelation, that man can know the true God of heaven. This divine revelation was imparted to the Jews.

Ronald Youngblood writes, "The Old Testament teaches that monotheism, far from having evolved through the centuries of Israel's history, is one of the inspired insights revealed to the covenant people by the one true God Himself."[77]

From God's creation of Adam (Genesis 1:26-31), to His walking with Enoch (Genesis 5:24), to the sparing of Noah in the flood (Genesis chapters 6-9), to the time He revealed Himself to Abraham (Genesis 12:1), God desired to lead humanity away from the faulty worship of many gods to the worship of the one true God. In the calling of Abraham God was initiating that through his descendants (the Hebrew people) He would have a people who were to be a light that shone to the nations the only true God (Genesis 12:1-3).

When one reads the Bible from the Old Testament to the New Testament, unity of the writers in regard to this monotheistic theme is evident. Abraham declared to the king of Sodom, "I have raised my hand to the Lord, God Most High, the Possessor of heaven and earth" (Genesis 14:22). This was an expression of his belief in only one true God in the face of tribal worship that prevailed around him.

The patriarchs were continually commanded by God to not become involved in the tribal polytheism of their neighbors (Genesis 35:1-4). As the infant Hebrew nation found themselves in Egypt because of famine, Jacob before his death admonished them to not become involved in the worship of the many gods of the Egyptians, but to stay loyal to the God who had revealed Himself to them (Genesis 49 and 50).

This monotheistic theme carries over into Exodus. Though born in Egypt, Moses recognized the uniqueness and oneness of God even though raised in Pharaoh's palace influenced by pagan priests. Events that unfolded in the life of Moses that found him on the backside of the desert, resulted in him encountering the Great I Am, who commissioned him to deliver the Hebrew children from bondage (Exodus 3:1-14).

Pharaoh's refusal to let the Hebrew children go led to the ten plagues, which in essence were the dramatic battle between the monotheistic God of the Hebrews and the many gods of the Egyptians. The victory by the Great I Am resulted in the Jews pledging allegiance to the revealed God of their fathers who demanded they have no other gods before them (Exodus 20:3).

God gave the Jews instructions in worship and living, and they were to attune their ears to His voice (Deuteronomy 6:1-25). Their daily declaration was, "Hear, O Israel: The Lord our God is one LORD" (Deuteronomy 6:4, KJV).

Eventually settling in the Promised Land, the judges and then the prophets were continually warning the Israelites to not stray from the revelation they had received (Leviticus 18:1-4). They were not to embrace the gods of their neighbors, but to embrace their duty and obligation to share the divine knowledge which had been revealed to them.

Throughout the Old Testament books from the Law, the prophets, to the Psalms they are all in unity in there expressions of the monotheistic revelation of Jehovah, whose power and wisdom overrules all other gods (Psalms 66:6-7; 139).

Isaiah reminds the people that the formed gods of men are nothing (Isaiah 44:10-11), and following them only leads to disaster. "For thus says the LORD . . . .'I am the Lord, and there is no other'" (Isaiah 45:18).

Jeremiah declared, "But the LORD is the true God, He is the living God, and the everlasting king . . ." (Jeremiah 10:10), and to follow the gods of man is falsehood and in vain (Jeremiah10:14-15). Unfortunately, the people did not listen to the prophets regarding their relationship with the true God and forsook Him to follow the gods of the nations around them (Jeremiah 2:19). As a result of playing the "harlot" with other gods, both the Northern (722 B.C. by the Assyrians) and Southern Kingdoms (587 B.C. by the Babylonians) eventually went into captivity.

The prophet of exile, Ezekiel, admonished the people to return to their monotheistic roots and seek God's forgiveness (Ezekiel 11:14-21). Once back in the land, prophets such as Haggai (1:1-15), Zechariah (1:1-6), and Malachi (1:1-14) warned the people to worship only the one true God of Heaven in order that the same fate would not come upon them again.

The New Testament also exhibits this same unity in regard to the monotheistic theme. Samuel J. Mikolaskl writes:

> The entire New Testament breathes the air of a monotheistic, creationist, and revelational basis for life. This is apparent

as much in the record of our Lord's life as it is in the writers' perspectives. The structure of both thought and language substantiates this. The structure stems from the Old Testament and is continuous with the revelation, with its promise climactically fulfilled in the life, death, resurrection, and ascension of Jesus Christ.[78]

The four Gospels picture Jesus as God's servant who came to restore man's relationship with the monotheistic God who had revealed Himself in history and recorded in the pages of the Old Testament. In a world of pagan religions Jesus taught, "The first of all the commandments is, Hear, O Israel; The Lord our God, the Lord is one. And you shall love the Lord your God with all your heart, and with all your soul, and with your entire mind, and with all your strength. This is the first commandment" (Mark 12:29-30). Jesus exhibited the same unity in regard to monotheism as the Old Testament did.

When Paul was in Athens he proclaimed a message at Mars Hill where there were gathered philosophers and worshippers of various gods. Paul tells those assembled to heed his message and not to worship god's made with the hands of men, but to worship the God and Father of the Lord Jesus Christ (Acts 17:22-34).

The other apostles, as well, wrote that worship and allegiance belong only to the one true God (Hebrews 1:1; James 1:1; I Peter 1:3; II Peter 1:1-2; Jude 25). It is to God, Father of Jesus Christ, who alone is worthy of our praise and obedience (Revelation 1:8).

It is plain to see, from Genesis to Revelation, there is an unbreakable thread of monotheistic unity, that there is only one true God, binds the sixty-six books of the Bible together. This internal consistency is more than the work of human thought or human construction, but gives witness to the work of the very God of whom the Bible speaks.

Moral and Ethical Unity

Second, there is moral and ethical unity that is a consistent cord visibly apparent throughout the whole of the Bible that attests to its uniqueness. From the beginning of God's revelation to man He let it be known the He was different from the tribal god's created by man's wisdom and hands. From the early chapters of Genesis we discover a God who is a holy, moral and ethical One. He is a holy God who has set standards and parameters for man's behavior in regard to himself and to others.

When one steps outside of the parameters of God's moral and ethical boundaries it creates unwanted consequences for the individual and others. This is clearly seen in the disobedience of Adam and Eve when they ate of the forbidden fruit (Genesis 3). It not only affected their lives, but those who would be their descendants as sin was birthed into the world (Romans 5:12). The God who created them set moral and ethical standards that were for their good and had their best interest in mind.

The polytheistic gods had no such ethical or moral parameters, as a follower of such gods lived without restraints. The Canaanites with their debased religious practices were a constant thorn in the moral side of the Israelites. Their system of worship was morally disgusting, as its participants sacrificed their children in the fire to Moloch (Leviticus 18:21), practiced homosexuality (Leviticus 18:22), and bestiality (Leviticus 18:23). Their moral behavior was so vile that it resulted in the Lord warning the Israelites to not associate with them and engage in such debased practices. The Jews were commanded by God not "to do according to all their abominations which they have done . . . ." (Deut. 20:18), "and according to the doings of the land of Canaan, where I am bringing you, you shall not do: nor shall you walk in their ordinances" (Lev. 18:3).

God's people were expected to adhere to a higher standard of moral conduct, and keep His statutes and judgments and "walk in them" (Leviticus 18:4-5). Such moral and ethical behavior was foreign in the religious practices of surrounding tribes and nations.

The Lord God of the Bible revealed Himself as One who demanded of His people exemplary conduct that respected others and upheld the integrity of the individual. The moral and ethical unity is a cord on which all the books of the Bible are attached.

Though Noah, Abraham, Isaac, and Jacob had their own weaknesses and failures, the Lord called them to strive to live by a higher moral code than others around them. Their ethical behavior was to be anchored in their relationship with the one true God.

When Moses received the Ten Commandments (Exodus 20), God gave the Jews a moral foundation that has been a rock on which down through the centuries has been sufficient for both individuals and nations to build upon. The commandments emphasize, first, man's relationship with God, and, second, man's relationship with others. This moral and ethical foundation has never been abolished.

Interwoven into every book of the Bible are the moral principles found in the early books of the Bible, giving witness to the Scriptures moral unity. Found in the Wisdom Literature, Proverbs, one finds advice on how to conduct and live before God and man.

In Psalms 119 the reader discovers the many benefits for those who walk in moral and ethical integrity. To love His precepts and walk in them is to live a life blessed by the Creator (Psalms 119:1-2).

All the prophets echo Micah's declaration when describing the walk of a moral and ethical person, "He has shown you, O man, what is good; and what does the Lord require of you, but to do justly, and to love mercy, and to walk humbly with your God?" (Micah 6:8).

The cord of moral unity continues into the New Testament, where we find Jesus expounding upon the moral and ethical conduct of a Kingdom citizen. Jesus elevated the moral behavior taught in the Old Testament, addressing more than one's conduct but the attitude and thinking that forms one's behavior (Matthew 5:21-48). For instance, Jesus took the commandment that forbade adultery and spoke of the misguided thoughts that leads to the act itself (Matthew 5:27-28). Taking the commandment to respect human life and murder, he addressed the emotion of anger that preceded the act. Jesus not only endorsed the moral laws of God, he raised the bar for Kingdom citizens to live radically different.

The Apostles express the same moral unity in their writings. Paul, Peter, John and James all admonish the Christian to walk worthy in the Lord (Ephesians 4:1), to abstain from immorality (I Thessalonians 4:3), forbids lying (Ephesians 4:25), stealing (Ephesians 4:28), pride (James 4:6), covetousness (James 5:1-3), gossip, (2 Thessalonians 3:11), bitterness (Ephesians 4:31), selfishness, speaking evil of others (James 4:11), and admonishes loving treatment of one's spouse (Ephesians 5:5:22-30).

Though there are some 1,600 years that spans from the first biblical writer to the last, all sixty-six books of the Bible possess a consistency in moral unity that is uncommon, even extraordinary. Concerning the moral and ethical unity found within the pages of the Bible, Augustus H. Strong writes:

> The perfection of this [moral] system is generally conceded. All will admit that it greatly surpasses any other system known among men . . . We may justly argue that a moral system so pure and perfect, since it surpasses all human powers of invention and runs counter to men's natural tastes and passions, must have had a supernatural, and if a supernatural, then a divine origin.[79]

Regardless of the prevailing societal values that exist; regardless of man's continual attempt to extend the boundaries of what is right and wrong; the moral and ethical unity of Scripture has been a light that neither time nor culture can extinguish. It is a supernatural light that transcends time and culture because its source originates in the eternal character of a holy God.

Christocentric Unity

Third, there is a Christocentric unity within the Bible that is the underlying theme and cohesive truth that amazingly binds and unifies all sixty-six books of the Bible together.

Every author has an overarching or underlying theme that runs through the whole of what they are writing. While there may be many sub-plots, an author's work is held together by a principle theme that unifies what they are writing.

So is it with the Author of the Bible, whose unifying theme is found in the whole of the Book. This underlying theme of the Bible is difficult to explain seeing some forty writers from various backgrounds over a period of about 1,600 years wrote the sixty-six books. What is amazing to the observant reader of the Bible is this undergirding truth unifies every book in the Bible. This reoccurring theme is not difficult to explain when one realizes the writers were chosen by the Divine Author to pen what He wanted revealed to humanity.

From beginning to the end, from the first to the last, from Genesis to Revelation the overarching theme of the Bible is Jesus Christ. The Bible through and through is Christocentric. While the Bible may speak of many topics and subjects, while it may speak of historical people and events or even touch on science, the Bible is a book of redemptive or salvation history. The Bible tells the unfolding story of how God worked in a historical context to bring into the world a Savior, Jesus Christ, whose purpose was/is the redemption of humankind.

J.I. Packer writes concerning the "God-guided unity" of the Bible, "It is more than a library of books by human authors; it is a single book with a single author—God the Spirit—and a single theme—God the Son, and the Father's saving purposes, which all revolve around Him."[80]

Jesus affirmed the He was the unifying theme that bound the Bible together. He said, "You search the Scriptures; for in them think you have eternal life; and these [are] they which testify of me" (John 5:39). After His resurrection Jesus explains that the whole of the Old Testament, the Law, the Psalms, and the prophets, spoke of Him (Luke 24:44). Christ affirms that it is He the Old Testament writers were writing about.

Christ being the underlying theme of the whole Bible, then it is Christ that binds the Old and New Testament together. Christ is interwoven into the whole of Scripture. In the Old Testament one sees Christ expected, in the New Testament one sees Christ explained. The key to the interpretation of all sixty-six books of the Bible is Jesus Christ. Christ's footprint can be seen in every book.

In the first few chapters of Genesis, one can see the beginning of the unfolding of redemptive history which purpose culminated in Jesus Christ. After Adam and Eve fell into sin, one finds the first promise of a Redeemer who was to come. In the hearing of Adam and Eve God tells the serpent, Satan, "And I will put enmity between you and the woman, and between your seed and her Seed; He shall bruise your head, and you shall bruise His heel" (Genesis 3:15). The promised Seed that was to come who would deliver a mortal wound to Satan would be Christ. God reiterates the promised Savior to Abraham in Genesis 12:1-3; 13:15, and that He would come from his seed.

Can one be sure these verses are talking about Christ? Paul in Galatians informs the reader that the "seed, which is Christ" (Gal. 3:16). Again, it is Christ who binds the Old and New Testament together. His face is seen in every book of the Bible.

From the promise in Genesis 3:15 onward God purposed to fulfill that promise. Further promises regarding the promised Savior were given to Abraham, for it was from his descendants that the Redeemer would come (Genesis 12:1-3). All through the Old Testament, one sees God is a redemptive God.

Examples of God's redemptive hand are only microcosms of the ultimate redemptive work that was/is promised in Christ. Pictures of God's redemptive power can be seen in redeeming the family of Jacob from famine and bringing them into Egypt to survive (Genesis 47:1ff). He redeemed the Hebrew children through Moses from slavery in Egypt (Exodus 3:7-10). Once in the Promised Land He is constantly redeeming the children of Israel from oppressors using judges and then later kings to do so. He redeemed Israel from captivity making it possible to return to their Promised Land (Ezra, Nehemiah). He redeemed Naomi and Ruth from a life of poverty by providing them with a kinsman redeemer (Ruth 4:14). He redeemed the three Hebrew children from the fiery furnace and Daniel from the Lion's Den (Daniel 2, 6).

While many more examples of God's redemptive work could be given, but then again, any and all examples given are pictures of God's redemptive hand building a foundation for the ultimate redemptive work that was/is promised in Christ. It is this redemptive promise found in Christ that illustrates and affirms perfectly the Bible's Christocentric unity.

A review of Christ's footprints on the books of the Bible shows an unmistakable unity that cannot be explained by mere human wisdom or reason. Looking closely one can see a divine Hand has left His fingerprints all over a work so completely and marvelously unified. In the Old Testament passages that follow the reader will find the redemptive promise or typology. The Old Testament is Christ promised.

In the corresponding New Testament passage the reader will find the redemptive fulfillment in Jesus Christ. The New Testament is Christ realized.

Upon examining Christ in each book of the Bible it affirms a remarkable unity that cannot be explained by mere human ingenuity. Let it be noted, in examining Christ in each book of the Bible, that while lists of this nature can be found in other sources, what follows is the result of this writer's accumulative knowledge that has been assimilated from over forty years of Bible study and research.

In Genesis, Christ is the promised Seed who would crush the head of Satan (3:15; Galatians 3:16), and the Lawgiver from the tribe of Judah (49:10; Matthew 1).

In Exodus, Christ is the Great I Am who spoke to Moses in the burning bush (3:14; John 8:5), the Passover Lamb (12:1-51; I Corinthians 5:7), and the Smitten Rock supplying water for the Jews in the wilderness (17:6: 2 Corinthians 10:4).

In Leviticus, Christ is the Sacrificial Lamb (chapters 1-10; John 1:36) and High Priest (chapters 1-10; Hebrews 5:5; 10:12).

In Numbers, Christ is the Star (24:17; Revelation 22:16), again, the Smitten Rock (20:8; 2 Corinthians 10:4) and the Brazen Serpent held up in the wilderness that brings healing to the people (24:4-9; John 3:14-15).

In Deuteronomy, Christ is the Prophet liken unto Moses (18:15-18; Acts 3:20-22).

In Joshua, Christ is the Captain of the Lord's host, a Captain of Deliverance (5:15; Hebrews 2:9).

In Judges, Christ is the delivering Judge to an oppressed people (Acts 10:42, 2 Timothy 4:8).

In Ruth, Christ is the Kinsman-Redeemer, the Lover and Protector (3:2; 4:13; Galatians 4:4-5), and the Seed in the lions of Obed (4:17; Matthew 1:5-17)

In I and 2 Samuel, Christ is the coming heir to the throne of David (II Samuel 12:12-13; Luke 1:31).

In I and 2 Kings, Christ is the One greater than Solomon (I Kings 10:1; Luke 11:31).

In I and 2 Chronicles, Christ is seen as the covenant maker (I Chronicles 11:3; Mark 14:24-25).

In Ezra, Christ is the Nail (9:8; Luke 24:39-40; John 20:27); Colossians 2:13-14).

In Nehemiah, Christ is the Restorer of that which is broken (2:13; Luke 4:18).

In Esther, Christ is the Intercessor and Advocate who seeks deliverance for His people (chapter 7; Romans 8:34; I John 2:1).

In Job, Christ is the Redeemer who ever lives (19:25; Galatians 4:5), and Mediator between God and man (9:33; I Timothy 2:5).

In Psalms, Christ is our Shepherd (Ps. 23; John 10:14) and the Crucified One (Ps. 22; Luke 23:33).

In Proverbs, Christ is our Wisdom (1:2; I Corinthians 1:30).

In Ecclesiastes, Christ is fulfillment of man's search (12:13-14; John 1:41; Philippians 3:4).

In the Song of Solomon, Christ is the Bridegroom and the Beloved One (6:3; Matthew 25:1-13; Ephesians 1:6).

In Isaiah Christ is the One born of a virgin (7:14; Matthew 1:18-23; Luke1:34) and the promised Prince of Peace (9:6; John 14:27).

In Jeremiah, Christ is the Branch of David (23:5; Revelation 5:5), and the Lord Our Righteousness (23:6; Romans 3:21-22).

In Lamentations, Christ is the Weeping Prophet (1:1-4; Luke 19:41-42).

In Ezekiel, Christ is the Son of Man (3:3, 17; Luke 17:24).

In Daniel, Christ is Stone made without hands (2:34, 45; Matthew 16:18), the Fourth Man in the fire (2:25; John 14:18), and the Ancient of Days (7: 9, 13, 22; Revelation 1:10-20).

In Hosea, Christ is Child out of Egypt (11:1; Matthew 1:13-15) and the faithful Husband (3:1-5; Ephesians 5:23-24).

In Joel, Christ is the Baptizer with Holy Spirit (2:28-29; Acts 2:14-21).

In Amos, Christ is the God Creator, He that forms all things (4:13; John 1:1-3; Colossians 1:17).

In Obadiah, Christ is the Ambassador sent among the heathen (v. 1; Galatians 4:4-6).

In Jonah, Christ is One who is greater than Jonah (1:15-17; Matthew 12:41-42).

In Micah, Christ is the Babe born in Bethlehem (5:2; Matthew 2:1-6).

In Nahum, Christ is the Wonder Worker that will not be believed (1:5; Acts 2:22).

In Hababbuk, Christ is the Lord's Right Hand (2:16; Acts 7:55).

In Zephaniah, Christ is the King of Israel, even the Lord (3:15; Matthew 2:2; John 6:15).

In Haggai, Christ is the Shaker of the Nations (2:7; Hebrews 12:26) and the I AM (1:13; 2:4; John 8:58).

In Zechariah, Christ is the One whom they pierced (12:10; Luke 24:40; John 20:17) and was wounded in the house of His friends (13:6; Luke 18-21; John 1:11).

In Malachi, Christ is the Messenger of the covenant (3:1; Hebrews 8:6) and the Sun of Righteousness (4:2; Romans 3:26).

In Matthew, Christ is the King of the Jews (2:2).

In Mark, Christ is the Servant of God (10:35).

In Luke, Christ is the Perfect Man, the Son of Man (1:1-3, 14).

In John, Christ is the Word of God become flesh (1:1-3, 14).

In Acts, Christ is the Ascended Lord (1:9-11), the One sitting at the right hand of the Father (7:55), and working through the Church in the Person of the Holy Spirit (1:8).

In Romans, Christ is the Justifier of the sinner, our Righteousness (3:20-26), and our heavenly Intercessor (8:34).

In I and 2 Corinthians, Christ is made unto us wisdom, righteousness, sanctification, and redemption (I Cor. 1:30); the sinners unspeakable Gift (2 Cor. 9:15), and the Victor over death (I Cor. 15:51-57).

In Galatians, Christ is our Freedom or Liberator (5:1), the Seed of Abraham (3:16), and the Redeemer from the Law (3:13).

In Ephesians, Christ is seated in heavenly places imparting blessings to His people (1:3), and the Head of the Church (5:23).

In Philippians, Christ is the One who was equal with God and humbled Himself to die on the cross for humanity (2:5-10), and the believer's joy (4:4).

In Colossians, Christ is the One who is the express image of God (1:15), the Creator of all things (1:17), and the Pre-eminent One (1:18).

In I and 2 Thessalonians, Christ is the One soon coming in clouds of glory to take His children home (I Thess. 4:13-18), and the One able to give peace (2 Thess. 3:16).

In I and 2 Timothy, Christ is our Mediator (I Tim. 2:5), and the God who became flesh (I Tim. 3:16).

In Titus, Christ is our Great God and Savior (2:13), and One who came to redeem humanity (2:14).

In Philemon, Christ is our Substitute who paid our debt (v. 6, 18, 19).

In Hebrews, Christ is the Sacrifice for humankinds sins (10:11-12), and the Author and finisher of our Faith (12:2), and the One who remains the same (13:8).

In James, Christ is Wisdom to the believer (1:5), the Unchangeable Father (1:17), and the Lawgiver who is able to save (4:12).

In I and 2 Peter, Christ is the One who bore our sins on the tree (I Peter 2:24), the Chief Shepherd (I Peter 5:4), and the One whose coming will be with power (II Peter 1:16).

In I John, Christ is the Advocate (2:1), the Propitiation for man's sin (2:2), and the One in whom dwells eternal life (5:11-13).

In 2 and 3 John, Christ is the Truth in which one should walk (I2 John v. 1, 3, 4; 3 John v. 1, 3, 4, 8,12).

In Jude, Christ is the Lord God (v. 4), and the Judger of those who believe not (v. 5).

In Revelation, Christ is Messenger to the Churches (chapters 2 and 3), the Lion of the Tribe of Judah (5:5), the Root of David (5:5), the Lamb of God (5:13), the Bright and Morning Star (22:16), the Faithful and True One (19:11), the Word of God (19:13), the King of Kings and Lord of Lords (19:16), and the Victorious Rider on the white horse, the One who will come quickly (19:14-16; 22:20).

That there is a Christocentric unity that underlies the whole of the Bible is indisputable. That Christ is the theme of each book of the Bible is unquestionable. He is interwoven throughout all sixty-six books. While obviously many other themes, topics, and subjects are addressed within the Bible, it is Christ who binds them all together (Colossians 1:17). Norman Geisler speaking to this issue of the Christocentric unity of the Bible writes:

> Despite the obvious fact that there are many other themes that intermingle with, and sometimes even dominate, the Christocentric theme of a given book, nevertheless, the overall theme of the Bible does not derive its unity from these other strands of truth. Rather, it is only because these strands of truth have been woven into the overall structure of scriptural truth about Christ that they reveal their ultimate meaning. The central meaning of Scripture is Christ, and therefore in a given book it is only the fact that its truth is related to Christ which constitutes that book's significance in relation to the canon of Scripture as a unified whole.[81]

Inspirational Unity

Fourth, the theme of inspiration is interwoven throughout each book of the Bible. The thematic unity regarding inspiration is prominent in both the Old and New Testament. The previous chapters, "The Bible's Claim," and "Can We Get A Witness?" examined the thematic unity relating to inspiration, so that information will not be revisited here. It was discovered that from Genesis to Revelation, one finds all sixty-six books contain within its pages a high degree of awareness that the Scriptural writings are divinely inspired. Suffice it to say here, as was seen, the prophets, the apostles, and Jesus affirms the Bible's inspiration with equal confidence and assurance.

Four major themes have been examined that are interwoven throughout the Scriptures that reveal a remarkable unity. The monotheistic unity, the moral and ethical unity, the Christocentric unity, and unity of inspiration are unifying threads that tie the whole of the Bible together.

When one considers the almost 1,600 year timeframe over which the Bible was written, and the vast differences in many of the geographical locations, their socio-economical and educational backgrounds of the some forty authors whose writings are found within, it is hard to explain by mere human logic how the themes of their writings are all unified and interwoven in all sixty-six books.

Coincidence it cannot be, but that a divine Mind guided the writers seems rather compelling in explaining the Bible's amazing unity.

CHAPTER 5
MATHEMATICAL UNITY AFFIRMS BIBLES INSPIRATIOIN

In the last chapter we looked at the first truth that gives affirmation the Bible is divinely inspired. Examining four facets of the diamond of thematic unity, it is obvious that such unity is more than the mere product of man's mind but the product of a divine Mind.

When it comes to the unity of the sacred text, one of the most remarkable truths found in both the Old and New Testament is a feature that most Christians know little about, many have never even heard of it. It is the Bible's mathematical unity. This amazing mathematical phenomenon is the second compelling truth that affirms the Bible's divine inspiration.

This most significant truth was thrust to a role of biblical importance by a Russian, Dr. Ivan Panin (1855-1942), who devoted fifty years of his life to Bible numerics. While he was not the first to discover that there was a unique mathematical structure that ran throughout the Bible, his lifelong devotion to the structure of its numeric order carried its study to a new level. His findings refute the claims of those who aspire to discredit the Bible's inspiration. His painstaking work of half-a-century affirms the Bible's uniqueness and the verbal inspiration of the Scriptures.

Panin was born in Russia in 1855. As a young man he participated in a plot to overthrow the Russian Czar, and as a result of his revolutionary activities he was exiled from his home land. First going to Germany, he eventually settled in the United States. He enrolled at Harvard

University in 1878, graduating four years later. He was known for his mastery of Russian literature and a gifted mathematician.

Philosophically Panin was a nihilist, believing that life had no true meaning or purpose. Finding no answers to life in nihilism, he later converted to Christianity, becoming a devout follower of Christ and His Word. After his conversion to Christianity he began studying the numerical pattern and structure of the Hebrew and Greek biblical texts. It was in 1890 that, as he said, "[I] discovered the phenomenal mathematical design underlying the Greek text of the *New Testament*."[82] He discovered there was a law of seven that ran throughout the Bible, which he claimed unlocked the numerical pattern that proved the Bible was divinely inspired. Such a numerical pattern could not happen by random chance, he argued. For the next fifty years he gave his time and energy to the numerical structure of the Bible.

Panin was a man blessed with an exceptional mathematical mind, as well as possessing a Christ-like spirit. Such a combination of mind and spirit found him being used mightily by the Lord. Karl Sabiers, author of *Mathematics Prove Holy Scriptures*, was an avid proponent of Panin's work, and also a personal friend of his. He wrote of this remarkable man:

> This distinguished person is a man of extra-ordinary resources in scholarship. He is keen-minded and alert and possesses amazing analytical and dissecting ability. He is eminently open and scientific. He assumes nothing, but bases all on observed facts, facts of a positive, irrefutable, unparalleled sort. He pursues his way with calmness and is positive of the ground he covers. His pleasing personality radiates the abiding presence of the Christ within. [83]

An author of many books, Panin's work, *Structure of the Bible*, was based on his numeric findings. At his death in 1942, at age 87, he left behind over 40,000 pages of notes. While many critics have not taken his work seriously or have dismissed his findings, no one has ever refuted his work or found such an extensive numeric pattern in other writings. His discoveries are to be taken very seriously and have withstood all critical examination.

Men look for scientific proof that the Bible is the inspired Word of God. Panin called his life's work, "the science of Bible numerics." His discoveries are mathematical proof the very structure, design, and order of the Hebrew and Greek texts are inspired by a supernatural Mind. Critics who reject and make light of his discoveries reveal the foundation of their unbelief is much deeper than the intellect. Skeptics find it much easier to reject his findings without attempting to examine them.

I was first introduced to Panin's writings back in the mid–1970. As a young preacher I read with amazement his discoveries. While there are those who are quick to dismiss his work without investigation, over the years I have read nothing of reputable quality that I feel can even remotely dispute the remarkable mathematical design he uncovered within the Bible.

Just what remarkable design and feature did Panin discover in the biblical text?

He discovered that every letter of the Hebrew and Greek texts is numbered and each occupies a unique place in the order of the total number of letters in the Bible. The letters in both the Hebrew and Greek has a numerical value. Each letter of the alphabet corresponds to a number. Numeric values are not given randomly to the letters, but are part of the Hebrew and Greek language. Since every letter has a numerical value, then every word, phrase, sentence and paragraph also has a numerical value.

He discovered that running, seemingly infinitely, throughout the original Hebrew and Greek texts was a law of seven. The number seven is a significant number in biblical thought. It is a number that speaks of completeness and perfection.

A reading of any English translation of the Bible one quickly discovers that from Genesis to Revelation the number seven reoccurs. God rested on the seventh day; there were seven years of famine in Egypt; the Israelites marched around the Walls of Jericho seven times for seven days, with seven priests carrying seven trumpets; the temple was seven years in being built and after its completion a feast was held for seven days; and Naaman washed seven times in the Jordan River. In Revelation the number seven occurs more than fifty times; as there are seven churches, seven lamp stands, seven seals, seven trumpets, seven vials, seven stars, seven spirits, seven years, and the list goes on. The Bible is divided into seven divisions: Law, Prophets, Writings, Gospels, Acts, Epistles, Revelation.

These are just a few examples of the many places the number seven is found in the Bible. The number seven is found in the Bible more than any other number. Again, it is well known by biblical scholars that the number seven is the number of fullness, completeness, of perfection.

What Panin demonstrated, by his countless hours of study, that the number seven, or the law of seven, is a mysterious phenomenon that is structured throughout the original Hebrew and Greek texts of the Bible. Panin, a master literary critic, studied other writings, but failed to ever find this extraordinary truth anywhere else but the Bible. He therefore contended, either the writer's of the Scriptures were amazing mathematicians, or each wrote as they were moved by the Holy Spirit.

Panin discovered, whether it is a book of the Bible, sentences in the Bible, or various passages of the Bible, that the law of seven is imbedded within. He uncovered the following kind of phenomena that exists within the biblical manuscripts. The number of words beginning with a vowel will divide by seven. The number of words beginning with a consonant will divide by seven. The number of letters in the vocabulary will divide by seven. The number of words in the vocabulary occurring more than once will divide by seven. The number of nouns will divide by seven. The number of words that are not nouns will divide by seven. The number of proper names will divide by seven. The male names will divide by seven. The female names will divide by seven. The number of words beginning with each of the letters of the alphabet will divide by seven.

Let us look at some examples of this astounding feature. Found in Matthew 1:1-17, is the genealogy of Christ. Dr. Panin found the law of seven running throughout.

A close look at Christ's genealogy in Matthew one finds, there were 42 generations from Abraham to Christ, or 6x7. The numeric value of the 72 Greek words used in the seventeen verses is 42,364 (6,052x7). The number of words which are nouns is exactly 56 (7 x 8).

The Greek word "the" occurs in the passage 56 times (7 x 8). There are two main sections in the passage: verse 1-11 and 12-17. In the first main section, the number of Greek vocabulary words used is 49 (7 x 7). Of these 49 words, the number of those beginning with a vowel is 28 (7 x 4). The number of words beginning with a consonant is 21(7 x 3). The total number of letters in these 49 words is exactly 266 (7 x 38). The numbers of vowels among these 266 letters is 140 (7 x 20). The number of consonants is 126 (7 x 18). Of these 49 words, the number of words which occur more than once is 35 (7 x 5). The number of words occurring only once is 14 (7 x2). The number of words which occur in only one form is 42 (7 x 6). The number of words appearing in more than one form is also 7. The number of 49 Greek vocabulary words which are nouns is 42 (7 x 6). The number of words which are not nouns is 7. Of the nouns, 35 are proper names (7 x 5). These 35 nouns are used 63 times (7 x 9). The number of male names is 28 (7 x 4). These male names occur 56 times (7 x 8). The number which is not male names is 7. The number of Greek letters in the women's names is 14 (7 x 2). The number of compound nouns is 7. The number of Greek letters in these 7 nouns is 49 (7 x 7). These are just a few of the many features in the passage divisible by seven.

Just examining Christ's genealogy numerically, the chances of all this being an accident is astronomical. Could this have happened by an unaided human mind? While Matthew was a tax collector and accustomed to dealing with money and math, it is highly doubtful he could have been that creative to make every feature of Christ's genealogy divisible by seven.

The skeptic might say all that is just a coincidence, a random occurrence. If it is, it is a huge coincidence that runs throughout every page of the Bible. The phenomenon that is found in Christ's genealogy is not limited just to those few Greek verses. Let us travel back even further than the first genealogy of the New Testament, and while traveling back, switching from Greek to Hebrew.

The first Hebrew line in the Bible is translated, "In the beginning God created the heaven and the earth" (Genesis 1:1). The seven Hebrew words have twenty-eight letters (4x7); there are three nouns (God, heaven, earth) with a total value of 777 (111x7); the one verb (created) totals 203 (29x7); the Hebrew words for "heaven" and "earth" have exactly seven letters; the value of the first and last words in the sentence is 1,393 (199x7); the value of the first and last letters of the verse total 497 (71x7); the last letters of the first and last words value 490 (70x7). Just in this one verse there are over thirty different numeric combinations that are divisible by seven. The chances of this being an accident is thirty-three trillion to one.[84]

When Panin's work regarding the phenomena of the law of seven, as found in the first seven verses of Genesis, was presented to some professors of mathematics at Harvard University, they attempted to disprove his findings. If they could, that would, as well, disprove the Bible's divine inspiration. After many attempts, they were unable to duplicate this amazing mathematical structure. Using the English language and assigning numeric values to the each letter, no matter what combination of numbers they used they could not duplicate this numeric structure. Despite their mathematical skills they were unable to recreate the multiples of 7 as found in the Hebrew words of Genesis 1:1.

In case one thinks this a contrived manipulation of the first seven words of Genesis 1:1, this phenomenon can be found in Genesis 1:1-5. The 33 Hebrew words used have a numerical value of 6,188 (884 x 7). The total value of the 33 initial letters used is 2,401, or 7x7x7x7 (or49x49). The 16 different initial letters have a value of 1,281 (183 x 7). The first and the last words in the vocabulary arranged alphabetically total 658 (94 x 7). The first and the last words total 924 (132 x 7). The value of every seventh word totals 1,008, which is (7 x 3 x 3 x 2 x 2 x2 x 2), not only a multiple of 7; but having seven factors which add up to 21 (3x7) Panin lists 14 more features of 7 concerning these first five verses.

It is truly astounding; the number "seven" permeates the whole of the Bible. The number 7 appears 287 times in the Old Testament (7 x 41), while the word "seventh" occurs 98 times (7 x 14). The word "seven-fold" appears seven times. In addition, the word "seventy" is used 56 times (7 x 8). The number seven speaks to us of God's divine perfection and perfect order. Could it be the Lord is trying to tell humanity His Word is perfect and orderly?

For anyone still thinking this is a coincidence, let us journey back to the New Testament and look at Matthew 1:18-25, the account of the virgin birth of Christ. The number of Greek words in this passage is 161 (23x7); the value of these words is 93,394 (13,342x7); the value of the vocabulary words used is 77 (11x7); found in this passage are six Greek words used nowhere else in the New Testament and their value is 5,005 (715x7); and these six Greek words have 126 letters (18x7).

Even if Matthew used his human genius to contrive this law of seven that is evident in his Gospel, how could he have known that the six words he used, that are found nowhere else in the New Testament, would not be used by other writers who followed him? We must assume the theory that he had an agreement with all the other writers not to use those six words, or he wrote Matthew last and must have had the rest of the New Testament before him when he wrote so he could use six words no one else did! Taking a phrase from Paul, "Certainly not!" (Romans 6:15).

Also found in Matthew 1:18-25, there are seven proper names in this passage; the numerical value of the name "Emmanuel" is 644 (92x7); the angel in speaking to Joseph uses 28 words (4x7); and the value of all the angel's words is 21,042 (3,006x7). There are many more examples of how the law of seven is found in just these eight verses.

Let us turn over to Mark 16:9-20, and look at his account of the resurrection of Jesus Christ. The law of seven is most prominent in this passage.

There are 175 Greek words in this passage (25x7); there are twenty-one verbs (3x7); the number of Greek letters in the vocabulary words is 553 (79x7); the number of vowels is 42x7, the number of consonants 37x7; of the 175 Greek words in the passage the number that are not part of Christ's words are 119 (17x7); the number of words used by Christ is 56 (8x7); and of the vocabulary of Christ 14 words (2x7) are only found in Mark. There are over twenty unique numeric features found in this passage that exhibit the law of seven. The chance of all these features being a coincidence is one in 27,368,747,340,080,916,343. [85]

In Mark 1:9-11, the number of words contained in the passage telling of Christ's baptism are 35 (5x7). The numerical value of the whole passage is 27,783 (3,969x 7).

In Mark 3:13-19, we find the account of Jesus choosing His twelve disciples. Interestingly, the names of all twelve numerically add up to 9,639, which is (1,377x7). In Mark 4:3-20, the number of Greek vocabulary words contained in the Parable of the Sower is 49 (7x7). In Mark 13:5-37, Christ's discourse on the end times, the number of words found in the words of Christ are 203 (29x7).

There are other interesting and amazing features regarding the law of seven. A few examples are considered.

The numeric value of the biblical books that are ascribed to an individual author, the total value of all their names is 7,931, which is a multiple of 7 (11x7x103). The numeric value of the Hebrew names of the twenty-one Old Testament writers is 3,808 (544x7). The numeric value of the Greek names of the writers of the New Testament is 4,123 (589x7).There are 847 references to Moses throughout the Bible (121x7).

Of the twenty-one Old Testament writers, there are but seven who are mentioned in the New Testament. The numeric value of the names of these men is 1,554 (222x7). The number of times these seven names occur in the Old Testament is 2,310 (330x7). The number of times David's name is found is 1,134 (162x7)

The Greek word "eternal" has a numeric value of 1,141 (63x7). The number of times "eternal" is used in the New Testament is 70 (10x7). Even the numeric value of all 70 times "eternal" is used is divisible by 7.

Concerning the childhood of Jesus, as recorded in Matthew 2, the number of Greek words used total 161 (23x7), the Greek letters total 896 (128x7), and the numeric value of all words is 17,647 x7. The numerical value from the words spoken by Herod, the Wise Men, and the angel are all divisible by 7.

The writers of the first and last books of the Bible, Moses and John have a numeric value of 1,414 (7x202). From beginning to end, the number seven is a thread found woven through all sixty-six books.

Still think all this mathematical unity is a coincidence? These amazing features are found from Genesis to Revelation. On every page of the Word the Lord has stamped the number seven, the number of perfection. If one letter is removed, or another added to the biblical text, this numerical structure is destroyed. How did each writer, unbeknownst to the other writer, manage to write in such a way that their words would contain this law of seven?

We have looked at just few of the thousands of examples Dr. Panin demonstrated regarding this law of seven that runs throughout the Bible, in every book and sentence of the Hebrew and Greek text. His results are mind-boggling numerical patterns featuring the law of seven that could not have been the result of human wisdom, and probability theory shows that such an occurrence being an "accident" is impossible. The answer seems convincing; God has put His signature and seal, the number seven, all over His Word, the number of completeness and perfection. What it all proves is that One divine, brilliant Mind wrote the Bible.

During Panin's lifetime he amassed over 40,000 pages of research regarding this mathematical phenomenon found in the biblical text. He once presented his findings to representatives of the Nobel Research Foundation asking them to verify his findings and conclusion that the Bible was unquestionably inspired. Their conclusion was, after a thorough investigation of his findings, the evidence was overwhelmingly in favor of such a statement.

Sabiers was privileged to personally examine and study much of the numeric data of Panin. After two and one-half years of pouring over Panin's findings, he succinctly wrote, "We have before our very eyes an actual scientific demonstration of the divine verbal inspiration of the Bible."[86]

Dr. Panin was so sure of his work, that he constantly challenged skeptics and Bible critics to prove him wrong. He publicly challenged atheists and rationalists to refute his findings, and to explain how this law of seven phenomena could occur in the Bible without a Divine Mind behind it. No one ever responded to his challenge.

In a letter he wrote to the *New York Sun*, which appeared in the newspaper on Sunday, November 19, 1899, entitled, "Inspiration of the Scriptures Scientifically Demonstrated," he issued a challenge to his critics. In commenting on the genealogy of Christ and birth of Christ, in Matthew 1:1-25, he wrote:

Let [a man] try to write some 300 words intelligently like this genealogy, and reproduce some numeric phenomena of like designs. If he does it in 6 months, he will indeed be a wonder. Let us assume that Matthew accomplished this feat in one month. The second part of this chapter, verses 18-25, relates the birth of the Christ. It consists of 161 words, or 23 sevens; occurring in 105 forms, or 15 sevens, with a vocabulary of 77 words or 11 sevens. Joseph is spoken to here by an angel. Accordingly, of the 77 words the angel uses 28 or 4 sevens; of the 105 forms he uses 35 or 5 sevens; the numeric value of the vocabulary is 52,605 or 7,515 sevens; of the forms, 65,429 or 9,347 sevens. This enumeration only begins as it was barely to scratch the surface of the numerics of this passage. But what is especially noteworthy here is the fact that the angel's speech has also a scheme of sevens making it a kind of ring within a ring, a wheel within a wheel. If [a man] can write a similar passage of 161 words with the same scheme of sevens alone (though there are several others here) in some three years, he would have accomplished a still greater wonder. Let us assume that Matthew accomplished this feat in only 6 months . . . It happens, however, to be a fact that Luke presents the same phenomena as Matthew and Mark, and so does John, and James, and Peter, and Jude, and Paul. And we have thus no longer two great unheard-of mathematical literati [intellectuals], but eight of them and each wrote after the other.[87]

While the newspaper in the following weeks received several responses to his letter, not one person could dispute his findings. The critics were silent in the face of Panin's masterful presentation of indisputable facts and figures.

When one considers the findings of Ivan Panin, it is impossible to simply dismiss his work without giving it serious thought and consideration. If one is to refute his work, they must show how it is possible for all sixty-six books of the Bible to contain the law of seven which is so intrinsically woven within. When you have such diversity in the educational, cultural, and economic background of many of the authors, how can one explain this mathematical structure? They are either coincidences, accidental, or they are there by design.

Skeptics have mocked Panin's "scientific mathematics" as illegitimate scholarship. They try to explain away his findings by arguing that Panin purposely altered the Biblical texts in order to fit the pattern he desired to achieve. Though they are quick to throw overboard his findings, none of the skeptics can prove he deliberately altered his findings, and they certainly cannot disprove the remarkable numeric structure built into the Bible. Their baseless and feeble charges are empty and without evidence.

If one is to refute the work of Panin they must prove his facts and figures are wrong. One must prove that his numerical findings are fabricated and he was dishonest and meant to intentionally deceive. No one has ever been able to prove his facts are wrong. What is amazing, his findings were computed before the days of computers, which reveal his brilliant intelligence and painstaking labors.

If one is to refute the work of Panin they must prove that the writers of the Bible were able to, by their own wisdom and ingenuity, accomplish such a feat. Panin even examined other classical Hebrew and Greek works in search of the same numerical structure, but he was unable to find this same feature outside of the biblical text. If one is unable to explain how the many writers of Scripture could accomplish such a feat by mere human intellect, then there is only one other conclusion to which one must arrive. The Bible is the divinely inspired Word of God.

Bible teacher D.M. Panton, commenting on Panin's discoveries, has written, "Verbal inspiration is here mathematically proven, past all cavil [doubt]. The Scriptures discloses itself as a parchment which, held up to the light, reveals the autograph of its Maker, a script that bears exactly that imprint of a miraculous arithmetic."[88]

Sabiers, wrote in 1941, the year before Panin's death, words that still hold true:

Every candid, logical minded individual is simply compelled to admit that the intelligence which planned and designed the Bible must have been Superhuman, Divine. That One Designer was a Supernatural, Master Designer. Only the Supreme, Omniscient, Omnipotent God could have caused such phenomenal numeric designs to occur beneath the surface of the Bible text. Only God could have constructed the Bible in the amazing manner in which it is constructed. The Eternal, Omnipotent Author designed, superintended, worked, and carried out His Own infinite plans. There is no escape from this conclusion.[89]

There is no human explanation for this incredible mathematical structure. The only explanation is that Someone with supernatural Intelligence guided the writer's, unknown to them, to pen their words based upon mathematical laws and structures that absolutely cannot be explained by human logic. The numerical structure of the Bible, as discovered by Panin, had to have been supernaturally designed. We must applaud and give praise to our Lord for His skillful handiwork.

As one ponders the mathematical unity of the Bible, the honest mind cannot help but come to the conclusion that it is truly a compelling truth that affirms the Bible is divinely inspired.

CHAPTER 6
FULFILLED PROPHECY AFFIRMS BIBLE'S INSPIRATION

In the last two chapters we have looked at the first and second compelling truths for affirmation that the Bible is divinely inspired. Looking at four facets of thematic unity, and then examining its mathematical unity, it was concluded such unity is more than mere coincidence or the product of human wisdom but a Divine Mind was behind the writers of Scripture.

The third compelling truth that affirms the divine inspiration of the Bible deals with fulfilled prophecy. This is one of the greatest objective evidences the Bible is more than a book that was born in man's mind but was conceived in the mind of God.

Before proceeding, the question needs to be answered, "What is prophecy?" Prophecy can refer to either a prophet forth-telling a message from the Lord or fore-telling the future. Commenting on the literal meaning of the word "prophet" Herbert Lockyer writes:

> [In Hebrew] *nabu* or prophet was an "announcer" or "herald" of the divine will and word . . . . *Nabi* is from a verb meaning "to boil forth" as a fountain, and represents one who speaks out freely from a full heart impelled by an inspiration from God. The literal meaning of the Greek word for prophet is "to speak forth" or "a forth-teller," that is, one who speaks forth the message which has been

communicated to him through divine inspiration, whether of practical duties or future events.[90]

A prophet's message could speak to the present situations and events within the community of people he was addressing, or his message could be predictive, speaking of situations and events that were to happen in the future. When the prophet spoke to the people to whom he was called in the immediate context of their lives with a message of encouragement, rebuke, comfort, instruction, or warning, he was a messenger of the Lord who was forth-telling God's message.

When the prophet, by the inspiration of the Holy Spirit, became predictive in his message he was fore-telling. When fore-telling, the prophet was predicting what God was going to do in the future, he was predicting events that were going to happen before they happened. In predictive prophecy the prophet was predicting history before it occurred.

It is the predictive side of prophecy and its fulfillment which will be dealt with here, as an affirming argument for the divine inspiration of the Bible. Justin Martyr, (ca. 105-165), one of the early Church Fathers, wrote regarding predictive prophecy and its fulfillment, "To declare a thing shall come to pass long before it is in being, and to bring it pass, this, or nothing is, the work of God."[91] A.T. Pierson writes, "Predictive prophecy is the foremost proof to which the Word of God appeals on its own behalf. It [is] the standing miracle by which God challenges faith in His inspired Word . . ."[92]

When a prophet prophesized about the future, he was not speaking out of his own speculative thoughts or opinions, but the "prophecy never came by the will of man, but holy men of God spoke as they were moved by the Holy Spirit" (2 Peter 1:20). Commenting on this verse Augustus H. Strong writes, "Prophecy is the foretelling of future events by virtue of direct communication from God—a foretelling . . . . would not, without this agency of God, be sufficient to explain."[93]

It will be discovered that hundreds of prophecies regarding the future foretold by the prophets were made centuries before they were literally and actually fulfilled. The fact they were literally fulfilled is an affirmation that the prophecy was of divine origin.

While there are many, many prophecies that have been fulfilled that could be examined, attention to the prophecies concerning Jesus Christ will be the focal point. As was seen in chapter four, from Genesis to Revelation the Bible is Christocentric. In the Old Testament one finds the progressive unfolding of God's redemptive purpose, which one finds in the New Testament was culminated or fulfilled in Jesus Christ. Found in the Old Testament are over 300 prophesies concerning the coming of the Redeemer, Jesus Christ. Strong writes, "The most important feature in prophecy is its Messianic element."[94]

Christ fulfilling those prophecies is not only the authenticating proof He was the promised Redeemer, but it affirms the Bible as being divinely inspired as those prophecies were fulfilled as predicted.

Concerning the hundreds of prophesies surrounding the Messiah, Pierson writes:

> Over 300 hundred predictions about the Messiah [are] to be found in the Old Testament. According to the law of compound probability, the chance of their coming true is represented by a fraction whose numerator is one and the denominator eighty-four followed by nearly one hundred ciphers. One might almost as well expect by accident to dip up any one particular drop out of the ocean as to expect so many prophetic rays to coverage by chance upon one man, in one place, at one time. God has put especially upon these prophecies as to His Son the stamp of absolute verity and indisputable certainty, so that we many know whom we have believed.[95]

Before looking at the literal fulfillment of many of the prophecies concerning Christ as found in the Old Testament, how did Christ view Himself in regard to Old Testament prophecies about the Messiah, the Redeemer? Not only, as shall be seen, were the New Testament writers fully persuaded that Christ was the fulfillment of the Old Testament messianic prophecies, Jesus Christ saw himself as the One in whom those prophecies found fulfillment.

That Jesus saw Himself as the fulfillment of the predicted Messiah of the Old Testament is confirmed by many statements He made. Jesus told a crowd who had gathered to hear Him, "You search the Scriptures . . . . and these [are] they which testify of Me" (John 5:38). He went on to say, "For if you believed Moses, you would have believed Me: for he wrote about Me" (John 5:46).

Visiting His home town of Nazareth, Jesus was worshiping in the synagogue and began reading Isaiah 61:1-3, which was a prophecy describing what the promised Messiah's redemptive ministry would be like when He came. He would "preach the gospel to the poor; He has sent Me to heal the broken hearted, to proclaim liberty to the captives, and recovery of sight to the blind, to set at liberty those that are oppressed" (Luke 4:18). Upon reading this portion of Scripture out of Isaiah He went and sat down, "and He began to say unto them, 'Today is this Scripture fulfilled in your hearing'" (Luke 4:20-21).

When Jesus was witnessing to the Samaritan woman at the well she was amazed at how much He knew about her. John's account reads, "The woman said to him, 'I know that Messiah is coming, who is called Christ, when He comes, He will tell us all things.' Jesus said unto her, 'I who speak to you am He'" (John 4:25-26).

While talking to a group of Pharisees, Jesus remarked, "Your father Abraham rejoiced to see My day: and he saw it and was glad . . . . Most assuredly, I say unto you, Before Abraham was, I AM" (John 8:56-58).

On the evening of the first day of His Resurrection, as Jesus walked with two travelers on the road to Emmaus, He "said unto them, O foolish ones, and slow of heart to believe in all that the prophets have spoken! Ought not Christ to have suffered these things, and to enter into his glory?" (Luke 24:25-26). Luke adds in verse twenty-seven, "And beginning at Moses and all the Prophets, he expounded to them in all the Scriptures the things concerning Himself."

In the Sermon on the Mount, found in Matthew chapters 5-7, Jesus proclaims that He had come to fulfill all that the law and prophets spoke concerning the promised Messiah. Jesus said, "Do not think I am come to destroy the Law or the Prophets. I did not come to destroy but to fulfill. For assuredly, I say unto you, 'Till heaven and earth pass away, one jot or one tittle will by no means pass from the law, till all is fulfilled'" (Matthew 5:17-18).

After His Resurrection, Jesus appeared unto His disciples, and said unto them, "These are the words which I spoke to you while I was still with you, that all things must be fulfilled, which were written in the Law of Moses, and the Prophets, and the Psalms, concerning Me" (Luke 24:44). Luke adds, "And He opened their understanding, that they might comprehend the Scriptures" (Luke 24:45).

It is clear from the Scriptures examined, Jesus saw Himself as the fulfillment of the Old Testament prophecies regarding the Messiah who was to come. Not only did Jesus see Himself as fulfilling the messianic prophecies, we find the Apostles in the Book of Acts preaching that Jesus was the prophetic fulfillment of the Old Testament. Peter preaching at Solomon's Porch, says of Jesus, "But those things which God foretold by the mouth of all His prophets, that the Christ would suffer, he [Jesus] has thus fulfilled" (Acts 3:18). At Thessalonica Paul proclaimed "that this Jesus, whom I preach to you is the Christ" (Acts 17:3).

Jesus attested to the fact that He was the chosen One to fulfill the messianic prophecies of the Old Testament, the Apostles affirmed that in their preaching, but can one be sure this man called Jesus was/is the promised Messiah? An examination of Old Testament messianic prophecies will confirm this truth, as well as affirm the divine inspiration of the Bible that made those predictions.

When this writer was in college many, many years ago, I became engaged in a conversation with a fellow student who professed to be an atheist. Believing the Bible was a book of man's making, he said there was no way anyone could prove the Bible was the inspired Word of God. Seeking to share with him the remarkable proof of fulfilled prophecy surrounding the life of Christ, the unbeliever remarked that it was only a coincidence and that Jesus knowing those prophecies arranged and lived His life in such a way that He happened to fulfill them. In other words, he was saying Jesus manipulated events to make it look like He had fulfilled them.

There is a major flaw in such reasoning, which was pointed out to him. Many of the prophecies dealing with the Messiah were beyond the control of Jesus to fulfill by arranging events to appear He had done so. For instance, the Old Testament predicted the place of the Messiah's birth (Micah 5:2), the tribe from which He would come (Genesis 49:10), the linage from which He would come (2 Samuel 7:12), the manner of His birth (Isaiah 7:14), as an infant being carried by Mary and Joseph into Egypt (Hosea 11:1), the manner of His death (Ps 22), that His clothes would be gambled for (Psalms 22:18), His piercings (Zechariah 12:10), no bones would be broken at his death (Psalms 34:20), and that he would be buried in the tomb of a rich man (Isaiah 53:9). It is obvious Jesus could not manipulate events before He was born or which surrounded His death. Jesus fulfilling such prophecies that were out of His control, as shall be seen, revealed He was truly the Son of God, the promised Redeemer.

In history there have been some forty men who have claimed to be the Messiah. However, it is easy to discern the truthfulness or the falsehood of someone claiming to be the Messiah. If they don't fulfill perfectly each of the prophecies that surround the Savior then their claim is false. In history there has only been one person who fulfilled all the messianic prophecies perfectly and literally. In examining these prophecies it will be seen, his name is Jesus Christ.

The first prophecy of a promised Savior, a promised Redeemer, is found in Genesis 3:15. After the fall of Adam and Eve the Lord says to the serpent (Satan), "And I will put enmity between you and the woman, and between your seed and her Seed; He shall bruise your head, and you shall bruise His heel." This promised Savior would be born like no other person, being born of the seed of a woman. All others who are born in this world are born of the seed of a man. The New Testament affirms Jesus as the fulfillment of Genesis 3:15, as Luke reveals that Jesus was conceived not by the seed of a man but by Mary being "over-shadowed" by "the power of the Highest" (Lk. 1:35). Paul sees the birth of Jesus as fulfilling Genesis 3:15 as he writes, "But when the fullness of the time was come, God sent forth His Son, born of woman, born under the law, to redeem those who were under the law, that we might receive the adoption as sons" (Gal. 4:4–5).

In Genesis it is found that of the three sons of Noah, the Messiah would descend from the linage of Shem. "And he (Noah) said, 'Blessed be the Lord God of Shem . . . '" (Genesis 9:26). The brothers of Shem were to be subservient to him. In the genealogy of Jesus found in Luke we find the He "was the son of Shem" (Luke 3:36).

Abraham, who was a descendent of Shem (Genesis 11:10-26), was told by the Lord in Genesis 12:1-3 that through him all the nations of the earth will be blessed and his "seed" will be blessed (Genesis 12:7). God later repeats this promise to Abraham telling him, "Also I will establish My covenant between Me and you and your descendants [seed] after you in their generations, for an everlasting covenant, to be God to you and your descendants [seed] after you" (Genesis 17:7). The Lord promised Abraham that in his son, Isaac, "I will establish My covenant with him for an everlasting covenant and with his descendants [seed] after him" (Genesis 17:19). The Lord tells Abraham again that "in thy seed shall the nations of the earth be blessed" (Genesis 26:4).

The promised "seed" was to be a descendant of Abraham and Isaac. Who was this "seed"? Jesus, who descended from the line of Abraham (Matthew 1:1), was that promised seed. Paul writes that Jesus Christ is the fulfillment of that promised "seed" who would bless all nations. "Now to Abraham and his Seed were the promises made. He does not say, 'And to seeds,' as of many, but as of one, 'And to your Seed,' who is Christ" (Galatians 3:16).

The Lord, through Jacob, prophesized that the coming Redeemer will come from the tribe of Judah and "the scepter shall not depart from Judah, nor a lawgiver from between his feet . . ." (Gen. 49:10). In Numbers, Balaam the prophet predicted, "A Star shall come out of Jacob; a Scepter shall rise out of Israel . . . out of Jacob One shall have dominion . . ." (Numbers 24:17-19). In Luke's genealogy of Christ we find Jesus was a descendant of Jacob and Judah (Luke 3:33–34), and John calls Jesus "the Lion of the tribe of Judah . . ." (Rev. 5:5).

The prophet Nathan told King David that through one of his descendants the Lord "will establish the throne of his kingdom forever . . . and your house and your kingdom shall be established forever before you. Your throne shall be established forever" (2 Samuel 7:12-16). Jeremiah prophesized that the coming Deliverer would be a descendant of King David when he wrote, "Behold, the days coming, says the LORD, 'That I will raise to David a Branch of righteousness;

a King shall reign and prosper, and execute judgment and righteousness in the earth'" (Jeremiah 23:5).

Jesus was that promised descendant of David who has legal right to the throne, as His genealogy from both Mary and Joseph can trace their linage through David. In Matthew, Joseph's genealogy, the legal genealogy, we see Jesus was a son of David, "And Jesse begot David the king; and David the king begot Solomon . . . (Matthew 1:6). In Luke, Mary's genealogy, the biological genealogy, we see Jesus was a son of David through his son Nathan (Luke 3:31). There is no question whether or not Jesus is from the linage of David, as He is a descendant on both sides!

Jesus alone is the rightful heir to the throne of David, the angel Gabriel declaring at Mary's conception, "He shall be great, and will be called the Son of the Highest; and the Lord God will give him the throne of his father David. And He shall reign over the house of Jacob forever, and of his kingdom there will be no end" (Luke 1:32–33).

The very first verse in the New Testament affirms that Jesus is not only the son of David, but a son of Abraham; "The book of the genealogy of Jesus Christ, the Son of David, the Son of Abraham" (Matthew 1:1) Paul in his Epistle to the Romans attests to the fact that Jesus was a son of David. He writes, "Jesus Christ our Lord, who was made of the seed of David according to the flesh" (Romans 1:3).

Isaiah, the poetic prophet, predicted over 700 years before Christ's birth that He would be born of a virgin. "Therefore the Lord Himself will give you a sign; Behold, the virgin shall conceive, and bear a Son, and shall call his name Immanuel" (Isaiah 7:14). Such a prediction would cut down on the possibilities of who could fulfill that prophecy!

Matthew wrote in his gospel that Jesus was conceived in the womb of Mary by the Holy Spirit (Matthew 1:19). An angel appeared unto Joseph, who was engaged to Mary, and in a dream said unto him, "Joseph, son of David, do not be afraid to take to you Mary your wife, for that which is conceived in her is of the Holy Spirit. And she will bring forth a Son, and you shall call his name JESUS: for He will save His people from their sins." (Matthew 1:20-21).

To further affirm the miraculous conception of Jesus, the angel assured Joseph all that had transpired was the fulfillment of prophecy.

The angel told him, "So all this was done that it might be fulfilled which was spoken by the Lord through the prophet, saying, 'Behold, the virgin shall be with child and bear a Son, and they shall call his name Emmanuel, which being translated, is God with us'" (Matthew 1:22-23).

Luke, as well, records that Mary was a virgin (Luke 1:27). Mary by her own testimony affirms that she was a virgin, as she asked the angel Gabriel, "How can this be, since I do not know a man?" (Luke 1:34). She is told the Holy Spirit would over-shadow her and the Child that would develop in her womb was to be "called the Son of God." (Luke 1:35). The Child she eventually gave birth to, "his name was called Jesus" (Luke 2:21).

While Isaiah predicted Jesus would be born of a virgin, Micah predicted the place where Jesus would be born. Micah, some 700 years before the birth of Jesus, writes, "But you, Bethlehem Ephratah, though you are little among the thousands of Judah, yet out of you shall come forth to Me the One to be the Ruler in Israel, whose goings forth are from of old, from everlasting" (Micah 5:2). While Mary and Joseph, who were living in Nazareth, were in Bethlehem registering to be taxed, "and so it was, that, while they were there, the days were completed for her to be delivered, and she brought forth her firstborn Son and wrapped Him in swaddling clothes, and laid him in a manger; because there was no room for them in the inn" (Luke 2:1-7).

Soon after Jesus was born, because of the murderous rampage of Herod putting to death male infants two years of age and under, Mary and Joseph took Jesus to Egypt until after Herod's death and it was safe to return (Matthew 2:14-21). Upon Mary and Joseph returning from Egypt they fulfilled the prophecy of Hosea which reads, "When Israel was a child, I loved him and out of Egypt I called my son" (Hosea 11:1). Of their fleeing to Egypt and eventual return with the Christ Child, Matthew writes that they were "there until the death of Herod: that it might be fulfilled which was spoken by the Lord through the prophet, saying, 'Out of Egypt I called my son'" (Matthew 2:15).

After returning from Egypt, Mary and Joseph and the Infant Jesus returned to Nazareth, where He would grow-up. This was prophesized by Isaiah, "There shall come forth a rod from the stem of Jesse, and a

Branch shall grow out of his roots" (Is. 11:1). Commenting on this verse Hebert Lockyer writes, "When Isaiah spoke of Jesus as the Branch, he uses the [Hebrew] word *neh-tzer*, meaning 'the separate One' or the 'Nazarene.'"[96]

In Matthew he records the fulfillment of Isaiah's prophecy. It says of Joseph, "And he came and dwelt in a city called Nazareth: that it might be fulfilled which was spoken by the prophets, 'He shall be called a Nazarene'" (Matthew 2:23).

The Old Testament is very clear as to how it is possible to recognize whether or not one is the Messiah. He must be from the seed of a woman, from the linage of Shem, Abraham, Isaac and Jacob, he must come from the tribe of Judah, the line of King David, to be born of a virgin, born in Bethlehem, and flees into Egypt for safety but returns to Nazareth to grow-up. There has only been one Man who has perfectly fulfilled these prophecies: his name is Jesus Christ.

To the skeptics who contend Jesus manipulated circumstance and events in order to fulfill messianic prophecies, it is an illogical argument. The prophecies that have been examined thus far that dealt with His linage, conception, and events surrounding his birth, show that it would have been impossible for Him to arrange those events. A more satisfactory explanation is that a Divine Mind planned it all and His hand moved in history to bring it all to pass just as the inspired Bible predicted.

In examining prophecies surrounding the Messiah's ministry, the life of Jesus fulfilled those as well. The Old Testament predicted that before the Messiah would begin His ministry a Forerunner would appear who would prepare the people for Christ's ministry. Isaiah prophesized, "The voice of one crying in the wilderness: Prepare the way of the Lord; make strait in the desert a highway for our God" (Is. 40:3). Malachi also predicted the Forerunner to precede the Messiah, "Behold, I will send My messenger, and he will prepare the way before Me: and the Lord, whom you seek, will suddenly come to his temple, even the messenger of the covenant, in whom you delight in: Behold, He is coming, says the LORD of hosts" (Mal. 3:1).

The fulfillment of Isaiah and Malachi's prophecies were fulfilled in John the Baptist. Matthew writes, "In those days John the Baptist came preaching in the wilderness of Judea, and saying, 'Repent, for the kingdom of heaven is at hand!' For this is he who was spoken of by the prophet Isaiah, saying, 'The voice of one crying in the wilderness. Prepare the way of the Lord, make His paths straight'" (Matthew 3:1-3).

Mark begins his Gospel with the predicted ministry of John the Baptist, "As it is written in the Prophets, 'Behold, I send my messenger before Your face, Who will prepare Your way before You. The voice of one crying in the wilderness: Prepare the way of the Lord, make His paths straight.' John came . . ." (Mark 1:2-4). Like Matthew and Mark, Luke also affirms that John the Baptist was the fulfillment of Isaiah and Malachi's prophecy (Lk. 3:4-6).

John the Baptist saw himself as the fulfillment of the Forerunner. When asked if he was the Christ, John replied that he was not the Christ, but "he said, 'I am the voice of one crying in the wilderness: Make straight the way of the Lord, as the prophet Isaiah said'" (John 1:21-23). Jesus, as well, affirmed in Luke that John was the fulfillment of the Forerunner, saying, "This is he of whom it is written . . ." (Lk. 7:27).

As John the Baptist's mission of paving the way for Christ was ending, he one day announced the inauguration of Christ's ministry, "and looking at Jesus as He walked, he said, 'Behold the Lamb of God!'" (John 1:36). John, in his statement, was acknowledging that Jesus was the promised Savior and the Sacrificial Lamb (Isaiah 53:7) who had come to die for the sins of the people. Hebrews affirms the Lamb of God John was referring to was Jesus, "But this Man [Jesus], after he had offered one sacrifice for sins forever, sat down at the right hand of God" (Heb. 10:12). Jesus, as the Lamb of God, offered the sacrifice of Himself on behalf of humanity.

Much of the ministry of Jesus, according to Isaiah, would be conducted in the area "of Zebulun and the land of Naphtali" and "beyond Jordan in Galilee . . ."(Isaiah 9:1-2). After the temptations of Jesus in the wilderness, Matthew records, "He departed into Galilee: and leaving Nazareth, He came and dwelt in Capernaum, which is upon the sea coast in the borders of Zebulum and Naphtali: That it might be fulfilled which was spoken by Isaiah the prophet saying . . ." (Matthew 4:12-17).

In Deuteronomy it was prophesied that the Messiah to come would be an instructive prophet like Moses. "The Lord your God will raise up for you a Prophet like me [Moses] from your midst, from your brethren. Him you shall hear . . . and I will put My words in His mouth; and he shall speak unto them all that I shall command Him" (Duet. 18:15-18).

Throughout his earthly ministry Jesus was seen as the fulfillment of "that Prophet" spoken of in Deuteronomy. After Jesus fed the five thousand, those who witnessed the miracle "that Jesus did, said, 'This is truly the Prophet who is come into the world'" (John 6:14). After Jesus broke-up a funeral by raising a young lad from the dead, those who witnessed this miraculous occurrence, "glorified God, saying, 'A great prophet is risen up among us; and God has visited His people'" (Luke 7:16).

In Acts we find Peter preaching a message that confirmed that Jesus was the fulfillment of the prophet like unto Moses. Peter preached the prophecy in Deuteronomy 18:1-19, that it found fulfillment in "Jesus Christ, who was preached to you before" (Acts 3:20-22).

The prophets prophesied that when the Messiah came His ministry would be characterized by the miraculous. Isaiah said that when He comes, "then the eyes of the blind shall be opened, and the ears of the deaf shall be unstopped. Then the lame shall leap like a deer and the tongue of the dumb sing . . ." (Isaiah 35:5-6).

As one reads the four Gospels it is evident the ministry of Jesus was characterized by such miracles as Isaiah specified. It was at a wedding in Cana of Galilee that "the beginning of signs [miracles] Jesus did . . . and manifested His glory . . ."(John 2:11). Those who witnessed the miracles of Jesus no doubt had the prophecy of Isaiah in mind when they remarked, "When the Christ comes, will He do more signs [miracles] than these which this man has done?" (John 7:31).

Even the enemies of Jesus who were plotting to kill Him had to confess to His many miraculous works. John writes, "Then the chief priests and the Pharisees gathered a council and said, 'What shall we do? For this man works many signs [miracles]'" (John11:47). The very enemies of Jesus, by their own admission of His many miracles, were affirming He was the fulfillment of Isaiah 35:5-6.

One of Christ's chief methods of teaching was using parables. Parables were earthly stories that sought to convey a spiritual truth. The Psalmist on two occasions predicted the Messiah would "open my mouth in a parable: I will utter dark sayings of old" (Ps. 49:4; 78:2). In Matthew one finds that Jesus "spoke many things unto them in parables" (Matt. 13:3). After Christ's discourse on the Sower He proceeded to teach with other parables. Matthew comments, "All these things Jesus spoke to the multitude in parables, and without a parable He did not speak to them, that it might be fulfilled which was spoken by the prophet saying, 'I will open my mouth in parables: I will utter things kept secret from the foundation of the world'" (Matthew 13:34-35).

Jesus, during his earthly ministry, predicted His death, but also His resurrection. When standing in front of the temple Jesus said, "Destroy this temple, and in three days I will raise it up.' . . . But He was speaking of the temple of His body" (John 2:19-22). In Matthew, after Peter confessed that Jesus was the Son of God, He began "to show to His disciples that He must go to Jerusalem, and suffer many things of the elders and chief priests and scribes, and be killed, and be raised the third day" (Matthew 16:21). A few hours before Jesus was arrested He told His disciples, "But after I have been raised I will go before you to Galilee" (Matthew 26:32).

While the disciples did not fully understand Christ's predictive words concerning His death and resurrection, after the fact His words were recalled. When He "had risen from the dead His disciples remembered that He had said this to them; and they believed the Scripture and the word which Jesus had said" (John 2:22).

Jesus, in predicting His death and resurrection, was fore-telling what David by the Spirit prophesized of the Messiah to come; that though He would suffer death He would not remain in the grave, "nor will You allow Your Holy One to see corruption" (Ps. 16:10). Peter, on the day of Pentecost, referred to this prophecy and the historical fact of Christ's death and resurrection being its fulfillment. Peter preached that Jesus, "whom God raised up, having loosed the pains of death, because it was not possible that He should be held to it. For David says concerning

Him . . . .'For You will not leave my soul in hell [grave], nor will You allow Your Holy One to see corruption'" (Acts 2:24-27).

The prophetic prediction leading up to and surrounding Jesus Christ's death, burial and resurrection are numerous and remarkable in their fulfillment. They all give testimony to the truth that Jesus was the fulfillment of the promised Messiah and the Bible which prophesized Him is divinely inspired.

As Jesus entered the last week of His life, before entering Jerusalem He commanded His disciples to go borrow a young donkey that He might ride into Jerusalem on it (Matthew 21:1-3). Both Isaiah and Zechariah predicted this incident (Is. 62:11; Zech.9:9), that has come to be known as Christ's Triumphal Entry. Matthew wrote of this occurrence, "All this was done, that it might be fulfilled which was spoken by the prophet, saying, 'Tell the daughter of Zion, Behold, your King is coming to you, lowly, and sitting on a donkey, a colt, the foal of a donkey'" (Matthew 21:4-5).

During those final hours of Jesus Christ's life He is betrayed by Judas, which was predicted in the Psalms, "Even my own familiar friend, in whom I trusted, who ate of my bread, has lifted up his heel against me" (Ps. 41:9). As Jesus shared a last meal with His disciples, we find the fulfillment of the prophecy. John records that as they were eating Jesus remarked, "Most assuredly, I say unto you, one of you will betray Me" (John 13:21).

Jesus, responding to the inquiry by the disciples as to who it was, said, "It is He, to whom I shall give a piece of bread when I have dipped it. And having dipped the bread, He gave it to Judas Iscariot, the son of Simon" (John 13:26). "Then Judas, who was betraying him . . . .," "having received the piece of bread, he then went out immediately. And it was night" (Matthew 26:25; John 13:30). Another prophecy relating to the Messiah was literally fulfilled.

Zechariah even predicted that Jesus would be betrayed for thirty pieces of silver, the money later returned to be used for the potter's field, a place to bury strangers (Zech. 11:13). Matthew records that after Judas realized what he had done in selling-out Jesus, he sought to return the blood money. "Then Judas, His betrayer, seeing that He had been condemned, was remorseful and brought back the thirty pieces of silver to the chief priest and elders" (Matthew 27:3). Casting the money on the floor they refused to take it back, calling it blood money (Matthew 27:5-6), "and they consulted together and bought with them the potter's field, to bury strangers in" (Matthew 27:7). Another prophecy fulfilled of which Jesus had no control.

After Jesus was arrested and false witnesses came against Jesus (Matthew 26:59-60), the prophets predicted the Savior would be physically mocked and beaten. Micah reveals that He would be smitten upon the cheek (Micah 5:1); and Isaiah that He would be beaten and spit upon (Is. 50:6). Matthew records, "Then they spit in His face, and beat Him; and others struck Him with the palms of their hands" (Matt. 26:67). John, as well, records the officers "struck Jesus with the palm of his hand" (John 18:22) and they mocked Him saying, "Hail, King of the Jews! And they struck Him with their hands" (John 19:3).

That Jesus would be crucified is portrayed in Psalm 22. The whole of the Psalm graphically describes the agony of one being crucified. The Psalm speaks of the coming Messiah's hands and feet being pierced (v. 16), bones being out of joint (v.14), tongue being parched (v. 15), and being mocked by those gathered (v. 13). According to Hubert Lockyer what is remarkable about this Psalm is:

> . . . death by crucifixion was unknown among Jews until their captivity, 600 B.C. The Jews executed their criminals by stoning. Crucifixion was a Roman and Grecian custom. But the Grecian and Roman empires were not in existence in David's time. Yet here is a prophecy written 1,000 years before Christ was born by a man who had never seen or heard of such a method of capital punishment as crucifixion. No other form of death could possibly correspond to the details David gives . . . [97]

That Jesus went to the cross no one disputes. "And when they had come to the place called Calvary, there they crucified Him" (Luke 23:33). "The soldiers also mocked Him . . ." (Luke 23:36).

While upon the cross, Psalm 22:18 predicted those around the cross would gamble for his garments. John 19:23-24 records the fulfillment,"

Then the soldiers, when they had crucified Jesus, took His garments and made four parts, to each soldier a part, and also the tunic. Now the tunic was without seam, woven from the top in one piece. They said therefore among themselves, 'Let us not tear it, but cast lots for it, whose it shall be': that the Scripture might be fulfilled, which says, 'They divided My garments among them, and for My clothing they cast lots'" (Jh.19:23-24).

Jesus was not crucified alone, two thieves were crucified with Him, one on each side (Luke 23:39-43). This was predicted by Isaiah who foretold that the Messiah would be "numbered with the transgressors" (Isaiah 53:12). Mark records, "With Him they also crucified two robbers, one on His right hand, and the other on his left. So the Scripture was fulfilled, which says, 'And he was numbered with the transgressors'" (Mark 15:27-28).

As one hung on the cross if the soldiers desired to speed death they would break the bones in the legs of the one being crucified. The Psalmist predicted that this would not happen to Jesus, "He guarded all his bones; not one of them is broken" (Ps. 34:20). While the two thieves crucified with Jesus had their legs broken, when the soldiers came to Jesus they did not break His legs (John 19:32-33). However, they did thrust a spear in His side (John 19:34), which Zechariah 12:10 said would happen. John writes, "For these things were done that the Scripture should be fulfilled, 'Not one of His bones shall be broken.' And again another Scripture says, 'They shall look on Him whom they pierced'" (John 19:36-37).

Matthew records that the last three hours Jesus hung on the cross there was darkness on the earth, from noon to 3 P.M. "Now from the sixth hour until the ninth hour there was darkness over all the land" (Matthew 27:45). This was the fulfillment of a prophecy of Amos, who prophesized that the Lord "will make the sun to go down at noon, and will darken the earth in broad daylight" (Amos 8:9).

Upon being taken down from the cross after His death, Jesus had no place to be buried. However, Isaiah predicted that the Messiah would make His grave "with the rich at His death" (Isaiah 53:9). Requesting to bury Jesus was Joseph of Arimathea, a rich man (Matthew 27:57). "This man went to Pilate and asked for the body of Jesus. Then Pilate commanded the body to be given to him" (Matthew 27:58). Joseph laid Jesus "in his new tomb, which he had hewn out in the rock . . ." (Matthew 27:60).

Though Jesus had been laid in a tomb and the doorway sealed, He had predicted that, "For as Jonah was three days and three nights in the belly of the [whale]: so will the Son of Man be three days and three nights in the heart of the earth" (Matthew 12:40). The prophecy that Jesus gave concerning His resurrection came to pass three days later, as "this Jesus God has raised up, of which we are all witnesses" (Acts 2:32). They may have "laid Him in a tomb. But God raised him from the dead" (Acts 13:29–30).

After his resurrection, Jesus "presented Himself alive after his suffering by many infallible proofs, being seen by them during forty days and speaking of the things pertaining to the kingdom of God" (Acts 1:3).

The resurrection was the authenticating proof that Jesus was the fulfillment of the long awaited promised Redeemer. The resurrection affirmed that God accepted the finished work of Christ on the cross as payment and satisfaction for humanities sin. Christ's earthly work complete, the Messiah was to "ascend on high" (Ps. 68:18) to sit at the Father's "right hand" (Ps. 110:1). The writer of Hebrews confirms Christ's completed work of redemption, "But this Man, after he had offered one sacrifice for sins forever, sat down at the right hand of God" (Heb. 10:12).

At the end of the forty days after His resurrection, Jesus was addressing a gathered crowd when suddenly, "while they watched, He was taken up, and a cloud received Him out of their sight. And while they looked steadfastly toward heaven as He went up, behold, two men stood by them in white apparel: who also said, 'Men of Galilee, why do you stand gazing up into heaven? This same Jesus, who was taken up from you into heaven, will so come in like manner as you saw Him go into heaven'" (Acts 1:9–11).

While the world awaits His return, He presently is "at the right hand of God, who also makes intercession for us" (Romans 8:34).

Space and time will not allow looking at all three hundred prophecies that could have been considered regarding the coming of the Messiah. Enough, though, have been examined that there can be no logical explanation as to all of them being literally fulfilled by mere coincidence.

As was said earlier, of the many prophecies examined, it would have been impossible for Jesus to have manipulated them in such a way as to fulfill them. In regard to the messianic predications, they only have perfect, non-manipulative fulfillment in Jesus Christ. Christ fulfilling the messianic prophecies is not only an overwhelming verification He was the promised Redeemer, but it is also a compelling truth that affirms the Bible as being divinely inspired.

CHAPTER 7
ARCHAEOLOGY AFFIRMS BIBLE'S INSPIRATION

Three compelling truths have been presented that affirm the Bible is more than a book born in the mind of man. The Bible's thematic unity, its mathematical unity, and fulfilled prophecy are three remarkable features that are reasoned explanations that validate the Bible's divine origin.

A fourth compelling truth that attests to the Bible being divinely inspired is archaeology. Archaeology has proven to be a valuable tool in verifying the historicity of places, people, and events found in the Bible that skeptics have contended are only a collection of fables, folklore, and fiction.

Before proceeding, what is archaeology and how does it relate to the Bible?

Donald J. Wiseman defines archaeology as "the study of antiquity."[98] Narrowing the scope of "the study of antiquity" to focus exclusively on biblical archaeology, he defines as "the selection of the evidence of those regions, places, and periods in which the peoples of Old Testament times lived."[99]

James L. Kelso, former Professor of Old Testament History and Biblical Archaeology, Pittsburgh Theological Seminary, states that biblical archaeology is, "putting life into dry bones, makes the broken pottery into whole and useful pieces, and brings the dead past and its inhabitants to life."[100]

Regarding the ongoing of archaeological investigations and discoveries, Frank E. Gaebelein writes, "[The Bible] is constantly being vindicated, as archaeology has solved one biblical problem after another, and as painstaking reexamination of [so-called] discrepancies has finally led to answers."[101]

The Jewish archaeologist, Nelson Glueck says, "No archaeological discovery has ever been made that contradicts or controverts historical statements in Scripture. Scores of archeological findings have been made which confirm in clear outline or exact detail historical statements in the Bible." [102]

The renowned biblical archaeologist, Robert D. Wilson (1856-1930), after a lifetime of specialized study in the Old Testament, has written, "I have come now to the conviction that no man knows enough to assail the truthfulness of the Old Testament. Whenever there is sufficient documentary evidence to make an investigation, the statements of the Bible, in the original texts, have stood the test."[103]

It was Wilson's contention that archaeology does not prove the Bible is inspired, it only authenticates that truth to be so; it only verifies the truthfulness of the written record within the sacred pages.

Harold Lindsell says, "There is sufficient evidence which has come from the work of the archaeologists to reinforce the Christian conviction that the Bible is an historical book, whose statements can be trusted."[104]

While the Bible's primary focus is not to serve as a history book, what it says about history is accurate. The Bible is a book of salvation history, the story of God working in and through history as He progressively unfolds His redemptive purpose which culminates in Jesus Christ. The record of God working in and through historical people and places is reliable and trustworthy, which archeology verifies. Examinations of a few of the hundreds of archaeological discoveries that have been unearthed over the years confirm with absolute accuracy the biblical record.

Shortly before the turn of the twentieth-century Julius Wellhausen (1844-1918), put forth a theory that the first five books of the Bible, the Pentateuch, were not written by Moses (Exodus 17:14), but were written by various writers several hundred years after Moses died. Even though the first five books claim Mosaic authorship, even though the prophets, Jesus, and the apostles attested to his authorship, Wellhasuen was insistent in his critical approach. While not the first to doubt the authorship of Moses, his detailed arguments held sway in the liberal camp for a number of years. If the authorship of Moses could be undermined, then that would call into question the reliability of the rest of the Bible. If the first five books are unreliable, then how is one to trust any part of the Bible?

Archaeological discoveries, since Wellhausen, have shown the fallacies in his assumptions and have affirmed the authorship of Moses. Liberalism contends that writing had not developed sufficiently for Moses to have penned the Pentateuch. Wilson, whose many discoveries have confirmed the remarkable accuracy of the Bible, uncovered written sources that reveal long before Moses there was in existence "a script in which to write; we know, also, that the Hebrew language was used in Palestine before the time of Moses."[105]

Gleason Archer writes that one of the most important archaeological discoveries that refutes Wellhausen's hypothesis was, "[The] discovery of the library of clay tablets discovered in the North Syrian site of Rases-Shamra, anciently known as Ugarit, in which were many hundreds of tablets written around 1,400 B.C. in an alphabetic cuneiform dialect of Canaanite, closely related to Hebrew."[106]

Archer points out these tablets not only contained government related documents, but there were numerous tablets dealing with religious matters. This discovery, Archer says, disproves the theory that "the Hebrews did not contrive to put their religious records into written form until a thousand years later."[107]

Wilson summarizes the results of these archaeological findings, saying, "There is no sufficient ground for believing that the Pentateuch did not originate with Moses."[108]

In Genesis 12 one finds the call of Abraham, born ca. 2166 B.C.[109] Growing up in Ur of the Chaldees (Genesis 11:31), critics once thought it was once a fictitious city. However, the archaeological discoveries of Leonard Woolley during the 1920's and 1930's reveal the city was advanced for that day educationally, economically, and commercially.

Archaeology proved the critics were wrong and verified the record of Scripture.

In Genesis 14 is found the story of Abraham achieving victory over Chedorlomer, king of Elam, and other Mesopotamian kings. Skeptics attacked the historical accuracy of this story, since no evidence outside the Bible existed to verify its truthfulness. Critic Theodore Noldeke called the story "fictitious" and Wellhausen labeled it a story that was historically unreliable. Even the renowned archaeologist, William F. Albright, wrote in 1918 that the story was a myth and was borrowed from other legends.

In 1929, as the result of Albright's own archaeological findings, the historical reliability of Genesis 14 was shown to be true, as inscriptions were found that listed the names of the kings that had been in question. Of his discoveries Albright confessed, though he at one time contended this story to be nothing by a legend, now Genesis 14 can no longer be considered as untrue because his finds confirmed the truthfulness of the biblical account.

Over forty times the Hittites are referred to in the Bible, yet for centuries there was no record outside the Bible that the Hittite civilization existed. They are first mentioned in Genesis 15:20. In Genesis 23:10-12 Abraham bought burial "plots" from a Hittite named Ephron. In Genesis 26:34 Esau married a Hittite girl name Judith. The Hittites are mentioned numerous times as inhabitants of the land the children of Israel were to overcome in their possessing the Promise Land (Exodus 23:38; 33:2).

The Hittites are mentioned up through the time of King David and Solomon. Uriah, who David had murdered after he committed adultery with Uriah's wife, was a Hittite (2 Samuel 12:9).

If a people are mentioned that many times in the Bible, one would think there would be evidence of their existence. Their only mention being found in the Bible, critics concluded they were a people who were of fables, folklore, and fiction; therefore, the Bible is unreliable in what it says. However, archaeological finds began to be uncovered around 1871 that confirmed the biblical record regarding the Hittites was accurate. In 1906-1907 numerous clay tablets were unearthed that gave further insight into the Hittite people.

Author of numerous books on archaeological discoveries, John Elder writes:

> One of the striking confirmations of Bible history to come from the science of archaeology is the 'recovery' of the Hittite peoples and their empires. Here is persons whose name appears again and again in the Old Testament, but who in secular history had been completely forgotten and whose very existence was considered to be extremely doubtful.[110]

Fred Wright, commenting on the archaeological discoveries regarding the Hittites, says, "Scripture accuracy has once more been proved by the archaeologists."[111]

The descendants of Jacob found themselves in Egypt because of famine throughout the earth (Exodus 41:56). They moved there at the invitation of Joseph, Jacob's son (Genesis 46). Joseph had ended up in Egypt because his brothers had sold him to the Midianites who in turn sold him to Egypt (Genesis 37:23-36). A path that led him from Potiphar's house, to prison, to Pharaoh's palace, Joseph was eventually put in a position next to Pharaoh to oversee distribution of food during a seven year famine that swept the land (Genesis 41:37-57). As the Hebrew children began to multiply in Egypt, and with the death of Joseph, there soon rose to power a Pharaoh who did not know Joseph (Exodus 1:7-10).

The Hebrew people were put into slavery and forced to make bricks for the "treasured cities" of the Pharaoh (Exodus 1:11-14). When eventually Moses requested of Pharaoh to let the people go, the hard hearted ruler responded by forcing the Jews to continue to make bricks, but making them without straw (Ex. 5:7). Is the Bible correct in stating that bricks were made without straw?

In 1883, archeological discoveries in Tell el-Maskhuta uncovered ruins of elaborate structures that were made with sun-baked bricks, some made with straw and some made without straw.[112] Archeological work from 1929-1932, at the site of Tanis, also discovered ruins of structures made with bricks that contained no straw. Once again archeology verified the biblical record was not fiction or fables, but confirmed the historical accuracy of the Bible.

In Joshua chapter six is found the story of Joshua and the Walls of Jericho. The Israelites were commanded to march around the Walls of Jericho one time for a period of six days, and then on the seventh day they were to march around the walls seven times (Joshua 6:3-4). Upon completing the march seven times around on the seventh day, the priests blew the trumpets and the people shouted (v. 20), and the Scripture says, "That the wall fell down flat. Then the people went up into the city, every man straight before him, and took the city" (v.20).

Scoffers contended that a wall falling down flat would be impossible; therefore, the story could not be true. John Garstang's archaeological discoveries of Jericho (1930-1936), found that the biblical record was true, and that the walls had fallen down flat just as the Bible said. Garstang writes regarding his findings:

> The outer wall suffered most, its remains falling down the slope. The inner wall is preserved only where it abuts upon the citadel, or tower, to a height of eighteen feet; elsewhere it is found largely to have fallen. Together with the remains of buildings upon it, into the space between the walls which was filled with ruins and debris. As to the main fact, then, there remains no doubt: the walls fell outwards so completely that the attackers would be able to clamber up and over their ruins into the city.[113]

The archaeological work of Kathleen Kenyon at Jericho (1952-1958), confirmed Garstang's findings regarding the walls of Jericho falling down flat. Once again, archeology verified the biblical record as true.

Wilson, in his book, *Is the Higher Criticism Scholarly?*, points out an amazing feature that attests to the Bible's accuracy. From his research he points out that when the Old Testament names or lists kings, archaeological finds reveal that those names are listed in the correct order in which they ruled. He writes, "We find that the Assyrian documents that mention the kings of Israel and Judah name them in the same order in which they appear in the chronicles of Israel and Judah."[114] He further adds, "That the names should have been transmitted to us through so many copyings and so many centuries, in so complete a state of preservation, is a phenomenon unequaled in the history of literature."[115]

The Old Testament records that King Hezekiah of Judah paid a tribute to the King of Assyria of "three hundred talents of silver and thirty talents of gold" (2 Kings 18:14). A record of this transaction was discovered when numerous Assyrian records were unearthed.[116] The Assyrian record stated that the amount of the tribute paid by Hezekiah was eight hundred talents of silver and thirty talents of gold, a definite contradiction to the biblical account. Of course, skeptics immediately argued that the Bible is in error.

Near the end of the nineteenth-century, archaeologists uncovered evidence that revealed that Judah and Assyria, while they measured the value of gold the same; they measured the value of silver differently. Sidney Collett writes, "It took exactly eight hundred Assyrian talents of silver to equal three hundred Hebrew talents . . . And thus, what was supposed to be a mistake, the minute accuracy of the Word of God was once more demonstrated."[117]

In Daniel the story is found of the aged prophet being called before Belshazzar to interpret some writing that appeared on the wall. Belshazzar told Daniel, "Now if you can read the writing and make known to me its interpretation, you shall be clothed with purple and have a chain of gold about your neck, and shall be the third ruler in the kingdom" (Daniel 5:16).

Critics were quick to label this an error, contending that Nabonidus was king rather than Belshazzar. Since there was no evidence that they were co-rulers, the biblical record of Belshazzar offering Daniel to be the third ruler in the kingdom is inaccurate. However, in 1854, writings were discovered regarding Nabonidus and Belshazzar, his son.[118] Toward the end of the nineteenth century archaeological findings revealed Aramaic inscriptions that described Belshazzar as king alongside his father. He was indeed co-ruler, making his offer to Daniel to be a third ruler a legitimate one.

This discovery not only verified the accuracy of the biblical record, but silences the critics who contend Daniel was written by someone other than Daniel at a later time.

Verifying further events that transpired in Daniel 5, was a discovery made in 1876, by Henry Rawlinson. Daniel records that the very night he interpreted the hand writing on the wall for the king, "that very night Belshazzar, the king of the Chaldeans, was slain" (Dan. 5:30). Rawlinson and his workers unearthed in Babylon over two-thousand ancient tablets. On one of the tablets was an account detailing the invasion of Babylon by the King of Persia.

Sidney Collett writes of the ancient tablets' account of the invasion:

> That Nabonidus first fled and then was taken prisoner; [the account] adds that on a certain "night . . . the king died." Now, seeing that Nabonidus, who was taken prisoner, lived for a considerable time after the fall of Babylon, this "king" could have been none other than Belshazzar, of whom the old Bible recorded long ago, that "in that night was Belshazzar the king of the Chaldeans slain.[119]

Once again, archaeology verifies the accuracy of Scripture. In this instance, twice in one chapter!

One of the greatest archaeological discoveries ever made was in 1947, with the "accidental" finding of what has come to be known as the Dead Sea Scrolls. The discovery was made near the Dead Sea in 1947, when a goat herder was searching for a stray goat. The original find of scrolls led to the discovery of more in 1948. The archaeologist W.F. Albright considered the archeological find to be the greatest discovery in modern times.

Over two hundred caves were explored in the area known as the Qumran community, with eleven of them containing either scrolls or fragments of scrolls. Found within the caves where manuscripts or parts of manuscripts of every book in the Old Testament except Esther. A complete scroll of Isaiah was discovered that biblical scholars estimated to be approximately 1,000 years older than any other known manuscript of Isaiah. Many of the manuscripts were given dates from the last century B.C., to the first and second century, older than any previously known.

Those who occupied the Qumran community were Jews who sought to be "sons of light" for God. They committed themselves to study and painstakingly preserved the writings of the Old Testament.

The importance of the Dead Sea Scrolls cannot be overstated. William Sanford LaSaor, writing on their significance, states:

> Prior to the finding of the scrolls, textual scholars, seeking to discover the earliest likely form of the OT text, had to work from a Hebrew text from the tenth century A.D., a Greek translation made probably between 250 and 100 B.C., a Latin translation made between A.D. 385 and 420, and other early versions. Now, however, for the portions of the OT recovered at Qumran, scholars have a Hebrew text from around 100 B.C. Early results in general confirm the accuracy of the existing Hebrew text.[120]

The discovery of the Dead Sea Scrolls was a blow to critics, as the scrolls established and verified the reliability of the Bible one holds in their hands.

In regard to New Testament archaeology, it, as well, confirms the historical accuracy of the preserved text. William Ramsay (1852-1916), one of the foremost archaeologists ever, at one time believed Acts was written by someone other than Luke, probably in the mid-second century. If Luke and Acts were not written by the same person, if that were true, which at the time he was convinced was, the writer of Acts then was not trustworthy regarding all the facts recorded. This brought into question the reliability of the New Testament record of the early church.

After extensive archaeological studies in Asia Minor, Ramsey's view changed. He became convinced Acts was written by Luke during his lifetime in the mid-first century. No longer skeptical of the historical accuracy of Acts, because of the archaeological facts Ramsey became impressed with Luke's careful attention to historical detail. From his studies he concluded, "Luke is a historian of the first rank . . . this author should be placed along with the greatest ever historians."[121]

In his work, *Was Christ Born In Bethlehem?* (1898), a book where Ramsey establishes the accuracy of the events surrounding Christ's birth, he states of Luke's writings (both Luke and Acts), "The account which Luke gives is, as he emphatically declares, trustworthy and certain . . . [and] states throughout what is perfectly trustworthy."[122]

Ramsey's conclusions about Luke's careful attention to detail are echoed by A.N. Sherwin-White. He writes, "The accounts of [Paul's] trials in Acts are so technically correct that Roman historians have often used them as the best illustration of Roman provincial jurisdiction in this particular period."[123]

Merrill F. Unger, archaeologist and author, summaries, "For Acts the confirmation of historicity is overwhelming . . . . Any attempt to reject its basic historicity must now appear absurd."[124]

Many more examples from the New Testament could be given where archaeology has verified the Biblical record, but only a few more will be considered. (Those who want to read more on the discoveries of archaeology as it relates to the verification of the Bible, are encouraged to read, *Archaeology and Bible History*, by Joseph P. Free and Howard F. Vos.)

In the eighteenth century, with the rise of rationalism, there was a school of thought that even doubted the existence of the historical Jesus. Did the Jesus depicted in the Bible really exist? After all, one of their contentions was that Jesus was not mentioned outside the biblical record. However, archaeological discoveries shed light on several secular writers who affirm the existence of the Jesus of the Bible.

Tacitus (ca. 60-120), a Roman historian, wrote of Jesus and those who followed Him. Pliny (ca. 62-113), a Roman governor, wrote of Jesus and the loyalty of His followers. The Greek literary writer, Lucian of Samosata, (ca. 125-190), wrote of Jesus being the founder of those who call themselves Christians. Jewish historian Josephus wrote of Jesus in his *Antiquities* (93) in terms that came close to attributing to Him divinity.

R.T. France in his book, *The Evidence for Jesus*, examines in detail the non-Christian, Christian, and archaeological evidences that without question verify the existence of the historical Jesus.[125]

There were critics who have disputed the existence of Pontius Pilate, who was governor of Judea during the time of Christ. However, in 1961 inscriptions that bore both the name and title of Pilate were unearthed in Caesarea, the Roman capital of Palestine.[126] Such a discovery quieted those who doubted his existence. Once again, the biblical record was/ is accurate.

The evening of the first day after the resurrection of Jesus, He appears to the frightened and shocked disciples gathered behind locked doors. As they gazed in awe upon the resurrected Christ, He says to them, "Behold My hands and My feet, that it is I Myself. Handle me, and see; for a spirit does not have flesh and bones as you see I have. When He had said this, He showed them his hands and his feet" (Luke 24:36-40).

Critics of the Bible contended that the Romans did not drive nails in the feet/ankles of one being crucified; ropes were used to tie and secure one's legs to the cross. If that be true, then the words attributed to Jesus was false and, therefore, the text unreliable, and Jesus, as well, unreliable. However, archaeological discoveries in Palestine have unearthed crucified individuals from the first-century which confirm that nails were driven in the feet/ankles of those condemned to the cross. This discovery verifies the trustworthiness of John's record and the words of Jesus.

Caiaphas, the Jewish high priest, is mentioned in John 18:13-14. It was Caiaphas who gave counsel to the Jews, advising them concerning Jesus as what to do with Him, "That it was expedient that one man should die for the people" (John 18:14). Those who thought that he was a myth were silenced in 1990, when "the burial grounds of Caiaphas, the Jewish high priest, and his family were uncovered in Jerusalem."[127]

Those who embraced the liberal theories of F.C. Baur (1792-1860), held to a late writing of John by someone other than John. It was his contention that the Gospel of John was not written until after 160, not in the first century by John as the early church fathers contented. However, the discovery of manuscripts and manuscript fragments of John validate the early date for John's writing and that John himself wrote the Gospel bearing his name. C.H. Roberts in 1935, after studying a manuscript fragment of the Gospel of John that had been unearthed, concluded that it was in circulation by 130.[128] Other experts in evaluating the manuscript fragment agreed with Roberts' assessment for an early date for the fragment.

Later, other manuscript fragments of John were discovered which evidence revealed they were in circulation by the mid-second century, still earlier than the 160 Baur set for the date when John was written. Archaeology verified the early date of John's writing and that John wrote it just as the early church fathers stated.

As can be seen just from the examples given, archaeology is a valuable tool that verifies the reliability and accuracy of the Bible. Time and time again, as one archaeologist has written, "Archaeology has confirmed countless passages which have been rejected by critics as unhistorical or contradictory to known faces."[129]

Clark K. Pinnock adds, "An honest [person] cannot dismiss a source of this kind. Skepticism regarding the historical credentials of Christianity is based upon an irrational [anti-supernatural] bias." [130]

Joseph Free writes with assurance:

> The accuracy and historicity of the Scriptures as God's Word and as his unique revelation has been denied by the destructive critic who has set aside the full validity of the Bible at point after point . . . Yet archaeological discoveries have shown that these critical charges and countless others are wrong and the Bible is trustworthy in the very statements that critics have set aside as untrustworthy . . . In summary, it may be said that two of the main functions of Bible archaeology are the illumination and the confirmation of the Bible.[131]

Gleason Archer writes about his confidence in the historical accuracy of the Bible:

As I have dealt with one apparent discrepancy after another and have studied the alleged contradictions between the biblical record and the evidence of linguistics, archaeology, or science, my confidence in the trustworthiness of Scripture has been repeatedly verified and strengthened by the discovery that almost every problem in Scripture that has ever been discovered by man, from ancient times until now, has been dealt with in a completely satisfactory manner by the biblical text itself—or else by objective archaeological information . . . No properly trained evangelical scholar has anything to fear from the hostile arguments and challenges of humanistic rationalists or detractors of any and every persuasion.[132]

Archaeology is a solid foundation on which to stand for believing in the truthfulness of the Bible for those who will honestly examine its findings. The Christian should not fear archaeology, but embrace it as a friend as continued discoveries give evidence to the Bible's trustworthiness.

Archaeology is a compelling truth that the Bible is more than a human book, but it is a Book that is divinely inspired.

CHAPTER 8
INDESTRUCTIBILITY OF BIBLE AFFIRMS INSPIRATION

From the beginning of time man has sought to preserve his thoughts and ideas by expressing himself through writing; beginning on cave walls, to stone tablets, to papyri, to parchment, and to paper. Whether it be the writings of such gifted men as Homer, Bacon, Shakespeare, Dickens, Burns, Longfellow, Poe, Twain, Frost, Sandburg, or Hemingway, their writings are hailed by even their critics as works of man's genius at its best.

As one approaches the Bible, an even greater "genius" is seen, a genius that is the result of divine inspiration. The author's of the Bible record history, poetry, prayers, man's highest aspirations, even his worst desires, and, of course, God's ultimate purpose of redemption. Instead of being respected and hailed as a great work of literature, even on the level of a Shakespeare or a Hemingway, it has come under attack like no other book ever written. The attack on the Bible is one that has been relentless and at times vicious. Yet in spite of the perpetual attack on the Bible it has withstood each and every one of them. The Bible has proven to be an eternal anvil that has taken man's hardest blows and is still intact.

The Bible's indestructibility in the face of attacks by critics is a fifth compelling truth for the veracity of the Bible as being divinely inspired. Uniquely, the Bible claims an unusual quality about itself that no other book can or has ever made. The Bible claims to have the intrinsic quality of indestructibility, that it cannot be destroyed.

Many passages speak to this unique claim. Isaiah writes, "The grass withers, the flower fades, but the word of our God stands forever"(Is. 40:8). Peter echoes this truth in the New Testament writing, "All flesh is as grass, and all the glory of man as the flower of the grass. The grass withers, and the flower falls away, but the word of the Lord endures forever" (I Peter 1:24-25).

The Psalmist declares, "Forever, O Lord, Your word is settled in heaven" (Ps. 119:89). In Psalm 19 he speaks of the Word of the Lord as being "perfect" (v. 7), "sure" (v. 7), "right" (v. 8), "pure" (v. 8), "true" (v.8"), "enduring forever" (v. 9). The Psalmist is asserting that the Word of God has existed in eternity past and will continue to exist in the future from generation to generation (Ps. 12:6-7).

Jesus attested to this intrinsic quality of the indestructibility of Scripture. He stated, "Heaven and earth will pass away, but My words will by no means [ever] pass away" (Matt. 24:35). In John, Jesus declared, "And the Scripture cannot be broken" (Jh. 10:35).

The Apostle John, as he comes to the end of the last book of the Bible, Revelation, warns not to add or take away from what is written for fear of reprisal on those who do. His wording of Revelation 22:18-19 clearly implies the eternal nature of what has been written.

One will search in vain for another book that makes the claim of indestructibility, that it cannot be destroyed. Yet, when one examines how the Bible has survived the continual attacks it has received, its indestructibly is undeniable. These continued attacks on the Book of books by skeptical individuals and groups are a reflection upon humankind's rebellious nature that seeks freedom from a relationship with the Creator, not one with Him. If the Bible is true, which is affirmed here, one then owes their allegiance to the God who has revealed Himself to humanity through His Word.

The Bible has been under attack from the beginning. As shall be examined, though the Bible has been maligned and continues to experience the hot breath of critics, it has in every instance come out unscathed.

Political/Governmental Opposition

As one journeys back through history, there can be cited examples of hostile political/governmental opposition to the Word of God. One of the first recorded instances of the abuse of the written Word occurred during the reign of Manasseh. He became King of Judah about 697 B.C., and ruled fifty-five years (2 Kings 21:1). "And he did evil in the sight of the Lord, according to the abominations of the nations whom the Lord had cast out before the children of Israel" (2 Kings 21:2). He led Judah into every kind of pagan worship imaginable, even sacrificing his own son to the god Molech (2 Kings 21:6). He despised the Word of God and led the people into abandoning and disregarding the Law of Moses. By the end of his reign a copy of the Word of God could not be found.

Manasseh's son, Amon, followed him and ruled for two years (2 Kings 21:19). He, too, "did that which was evil in the sight of the Lord" (2 Kings 21:20). Servants in the palace conspired against Amon and slew him, and in his stead made Josiah, his son, king (2 Kings 21:23-26). Josiah was only eight years old when he came to the throne, but he sought to do that which was right in the sight of the Lord (2 King 22:1-12).

The light of the Word of the Lord had seemingly been extinguished from the land. However, in the eighteenth year of the reign of Josiah, Hiklah, the high priest, while doing repairs on the Temple, found a copy of the Word of God (2 Kings 22:3-8). Upon hearing it read to him, the king wept (2 Kings 22:11). Josiah sought to lead the people into obeying the Scriptures, and as a result, the Lord promised him that Judah would receive a temporary reprieve before Babylonian captivity would occur (2 Kings 22:15-20).

While Manasseh and Amon had sought to rid the land of the Word of God and obedience to it, because of its indestructible quality it arose from the dust and ruins of the temple to bring revival to the land.

In the waning days of the Southern Kingdom, we find Jeremiah sending a copy of the Word of the Lord, which had been given to him, to King Jehoiakim. As it was read to the king, "Now the king was sitting in the winter house in the ninth month, with a fire burning on the hearth burning before him. And it happened, when Jehudia had read three or four columns, that the king cut it with the scribe's knife, until all the scroll was consumed in the fire that was on the hearth" (Jer. 36:22-23).

God's Word, though, is forever settled in heaven. "Then Jeremiah took another scroll and gave to Baruch the scribe, the son of Neriah, who wrote on it the instruction of Jeremiah all the words of the book which Jehoiakim king of Judah had burned in the fire" (Jeremiah 36:32). The fire of the king could not destroy that which is/was indestructible.

One of the most evil rulers in history, whose intentions were to destroy every existing copy of the Word of God, was Antiochus Epiphanes (215 B.C.-164 B.C). As the result of the empire of Alexander the Great being divided into four divisions at his death (323 B.C.), in the process of time the Jews eventually fell under the rule of Antiochus Epiphanes (175 B.C.). He horribly persecuted the Jewish people, murdering multitudes of them and doing all he could to destroy the Old Testament writings.

Found written in the *Apocrypha* is a record of his attack on the Scriptures, "The books of the law which they [the officials of Antiochus] found they tore to pieces and burned with fire. Where the book of the covenant was found in the possession of any one, or if any one adhered to the laws, the decree of the king condemned him to death"[133] (I Maccabeus 1:56-57).

Josephus, the first-century Jewish historian, wrote in *Antiquities* of this horrible time in Jewish history, "And if there were any sacred book of the law found, it was destroyed, and those [Jews] with whom they were found miserably perished also" (12.5.4).[134] However, through a revolt led by Matthias, and later, his son, Judas Maccabeus, the Jewish people defeated Antiochus' forces. The Jews upon gaining victory cleansed the Temple, and sought to reestablish obedience to the Word of God. The extreme persecution of God's people and the attempt to destroy the Scriptures gave evidence once again to the indestructibleness of the Scriptures.

At the time of Christ's birth the Roman Empire was ruling. Herod, who was a puppet of Rome, tried to stop Christianity before it even started. Upon hearing from the Wise Men that the "King of Jews" had been born, he attempted to slay all male children two years of age and under in an effort to stop this new born King from rivaling his power (Matthew 2:16-18). God spoke to Mary and Joseph to take the child to Egypt until Herod died, then they could return back home (Matthew 2:3-21). The attempt to destroy the living Word failed; just as trying to destroy the written Word will fail.

After His resurrection and through the missionary work of Paul, Christianity began to spread through the Roman world. While there was persecution of Christians from the various Roman emperors who came to power, none was more vicious in their persecution than Diocletian (284-305). On February 23, 303, he issued an edict which was for the purpose of not only exterminating Christians, but burning every copy of the Scriptures.[135]

Diocletian declared Christians outlaws and seized all the copies of the sacred volume he could find and had them burned. The wicked emperor boasted, "I have completely exterminated the Christian writings from the face of the earth."[136] While many Christians were martyred, and many copies of the Scriptures burned, Diocletian's plan to rid the earth of all Christians and their Book failed.

Upon Diocletian's death in 305, Constantine came to power. Becoming a Christian, in 313 he issued a decree giving protection to the followers of Christ. Declaring "the Bible as the Infallible Judge of Truth," he even had the government reproduce copies of the Scriptures to be used in churches.[137] In less than ten years after Diocletian sought to purge the earth of the Bible, it was declared to be the standard of truth!

Persecution against Christians and the Bible heated up again in 361 when Julian became the Roman ruler. As soon as he ascended to the throne he sought to persecute Christians and rid the empire of the Bible. His hostility toward the Bible earned him the name Julian the Apostate. His rampage against Christianity and the Bible only lasted two years, as he was killed in a battle in 363, and even while he lay dying he uttered the most horrible of blasphemies. His persecution backfired, as it resulted in the spread of Christianity and the Bible; as Jovian who followed Julian gave Christians more freedom. Julian died trying to destroy that which is indestructible.

Ecclesiastical Opposition

After the collapse of the Western Roman Empire in 476, and with the dawn of what historians call the Middle Ages, which was a period of time of about a thousand years from the fifth century to the fifteenth century, there was opposition to the circulation of the Bible. As the Roman Catholic Church gained dominance in ecclesiastical matters, they suppressed and discouraged the common person from reading the Bible, teaching that interpreting what the Bible says should be left to the priests. As the papal system became more and more corrupt they sought even the more to keep the Bible from the people, teaching more the traditions and dogmas of the church which kept the populace prisoners to papal authority.

Efforts were made to keep the Scriptures hidden and locked-away from the populace, and when someone was found with a copy of the Bible it was confiscated and burned. The church avowed that anyone caught reading the Bible or in possession of a Bible, "without . . . permission may not receive absolution from their sins till they have handed [the copies of Scriptures] over . . ."[138] This was a period of dark ages as it sought to keep the Bible in the dark, hidden from society.

When a layperson did happen to obtain of a copy of the Bible and read it, it shed Light on the corruption of the papacy. If someone spoke against the corruptions of the Roman Church, they were silenced by death and their copy of the Bible destroyed. Preaching anything other than church theology and anywhere other than controlled church settings was forbidden. Many sobering accounts can be found in *Fox's Book of Martyrs* of persons who were hanged, drowned, or burned at the stake during the Middle Ages for preaching from the Scriptures and refusing to adhere to the traditions of the Roman Church.[139]

In the eleventh century, a group of believers, who as the result of obtaining a copy of the Scriptures and upon reading the Word, began a movement which desired to see reform within the church. They believed that spiritual authority was derived from Scripture alone and not from the Roman Church. The church sought to silence them, with many going underground and others being executed. They laid a foundation and planted seeds for a greater Reformation to come, where the Word would not be hid but widely circulated.

Born in England around 1324 was John Wycliffe, who has been called by historians "the Morning Star of the Reformation." Receiving his education at Oxford, he became a university professor. He became disturbed at the low spiritual state and corruption within the Roman Church and desired to see reform, but his cries fell on deaf ears. Because of his outspokenness against the corruption he saw in the church, Wycliffe was put on trial in order to silence him. He was told to cease his teaching and preaching against the papacy, but instead of keeping quiet, he became more outspoken.

His greatest contribution was his passion to see the Bible translated into English and made available to the populace. Using the Latin Vulgate, he embarked upon the painstaking task of translating the Bible into the common language of the people. The church sought to suppress his efforts to make the Bible available in English. However, by 1384, his task was completed.

While the Roman Church sought to suppress Wycliffe's translation from finding its way into the hands of the populace, their opposing it had the opposite effect as people were hungry for a copy. The printing press had not yet been invented so copies were laboriously made by hand. It was available for sale to those who could afford it and those who could not purchase the whole Bible could purchase selected portions of the Gospels and Epistles.

Wycliffe's work was labeled as heresy, but he died (1386) before any official action could be taken against him. His work started a fire that could not be extinguished, as the followers of Wycliffe continued the work he started. John Purvey revised Wycliffe's translation and the Bible continued to slowly make its way into the hands of the people. Purvey was later put in prison for his continuing to provide the Bible to the public.

A decree was issued in 1408 that no one could translate or read the Bible without incurring the wrath of the Roman Catholic Church. The Roman Church so detested what Wycliffe had done, that forty years after his death they dug up his body, burned his bones and scattered his ashes. The church had hoped their detestable act would erase the name of Wycliffe from the minds of the people. To the church's dismay, the fire of the Word of God could and cannot be extinguished.

With the invention of the printing press in the 1450's, the Bible for the first time could be mass produced instead of hand copied, which made it possible to get more copies into the hands of the laypeople.

The writings and work of Wycliffe influenced a man in Bohemia named John Huss (1369-1415). Ordained a priest in 1400, the Czech priest was influenced by the writings of Wycliffe and began speaking out against the corruption and false teachings of the papacy. His efforts to spread the teaching and writings of Wycliffe became a fire that the papacy could not stop. The church condemned the writings of Wycliffe and when his works were found they were burned. To the consternation of Rome, Huss continued to preach that Christ and the Bible were to be the authority of the Church and the individual.

Huss was told to cease his preaching against the papacy or face severe consequences. He only became bolder. Summoned in 1414 to appear before the Council of Constance, he was asked to recant his teachings. When he refused to recant, he was labeled a heretic and sentenced to burn at the stake.

On July 6, 1415, Huss was burned at the stake, but the fire of the Word of God cannot be contained. Though the papacy had tried to imprison the Bible under lock and key, their efforts failed as the Word cannot be bound (2 Timothy 2:9). His last words were reported to be, "You are now going to burn a goose, but in a century you will have a swan which you can neither roast nor boil." [140]

The last words of Huss proved to be prophetic, as the fire of the Word continued to spread from England to Bohemia, and making its way into Germany where it became a blaze that became uncontainable. The fires of man cannot destroy the eternal Word.

In Germany, a monk named Martin Luther (1483-1546), was struggling to find inward peace, as the traditions and rites of the church left him empty. He would become the swan Huss had predicted.

Luther's inward despair led him to the Bible, where his eyes fell upon a passage in Romans, "For therein is the righteousness of God revealed from faith to faith; as it is written, The just shall live by faith" (Romans 1:17, KJV). The truth contained in the verse finally found its way into his heart. Luther realized that righteousness could not be earned as taught by the Roman Church, that Christ was his righteousness which was received by faith.

Luther realized his new found faith in Christ contradicted the teaching of Rome. Desiring to see reform within the church, he nailed ninety-five theses on the church door at Wittenberg on October 31, 1517. The accusations he brought against the church, and Luther's demand for reform, gave birth to the Reformation.

Luther could not be silenced, and on January 3, 1521, the Pope excommunicated him and declared him to be a heretic. On April 18, 1521, he was summoned to the Diet of Worms and asked to recant his teachings and writings. Luther responded by saying, "Unless I am convinced by proofs from Scriptures or by plain and clear reason and arguments, I can and will not retract, for it is neither safe nor wise to do anything against conscience. Here I stand. I can do no other. God help me."[141]

Declared an outlaw, Luther continued protesting the abuses and anti-biblical practices of the Roman Church until his death in 1546. Luther contended the Bible was to be solely the rule for faith and practice, Sola Scriptura, not the traditions of the Roman Church. Zwingli (1484-1531), in Switzerland, echoed Luther's high regard for the Bible; and then John Calvin, a second generation Reformer, in his *Institutes*, thoroughly sought to examine and explain what the Bible taught on matters of faith and practice.

In England the fire that was ignited by Wycliffe was growing larger, as William Tyndale translated the Greek New Testament into English. Wycliffe had used the Latin Vulgate for his version. Tyndale used the original Greek text in his translation that had been published by Erasmus (1516). Because of economic reasons and his endeavors being frowned upon by the church, he left England and went to Germany. Befriended by Luther, in 1525 he had three thousand copies printed of the New Testament in English. There was such a demand in England six more additions were printed, numbering in all about fifteen thousand copies. They had to be smuggled into England.

The papacy burned every copy they could find trying to stop its spread, but it was a fire that could not be extinguished. Tyndale, who was considered an enemy of the papacy, was eventually captured in

Belgium. He was declared to be a heretic, and in 1536 he was strangled and his body burned at the stake.

Though Tyndale had been executed it didn't stop the spread of the Word of God. With England's break from the Roman Catholic Church in 1534, a more favorable atmosphere was slowly developing toward Protestants, which resulted in more English translations appearing in England. The Coverdale Bible was published in 1535 by Miles Coverdale and the Matthew's Bible in 1537 by John Rodgers. All of this was done with King Henry VIII's permission. This was followed in 1539 by the Great Bible, which was a revision of the Coverdale Bible, it was known for its large print size. However, toward the end of his reign the king became hostile toward proponents of the Tyndale New Testament and Coverdale Bible, sanctioning only the reading of the Great Bible. Eventually banning the reading of both, he burned all he could confiscate.

Upon Henry VIII's death in 1547, Edward VI came to the throne and encouraged the reading of the Bible and had the Great Bible placed in every church. The reprieve, though, was short lived.

When Queen Mary Tudor came to the English throne in 1553, she was hostile to the Protestant movement, and many Christians lost their lives, including many who were associated with Bible translations. Many fled to Geneva, which was under the leadership of John Calvin. In 1560, William Whittingham, brother-in-law to Calvin, produced an English translation called the Geneva Bible. The Bible went through 160 editions. Mary's hostile reign lasted less than four years, yet the spread of the Bible marched on.

When Queen Elizabeth ascended the throne in 1557, she encouraged the people to read the Bible and, like Edward VI, once again had the Great Bible placed in every church. During her reign several new English translations appeared: The Bishop's Bible (1568), and the Martin Bible (1582).

King James I ascended the throne in 1603, and immediately suggested a new translation of the Bible be produced. After meeting with various church leaders, it was decided that a new translation would be published based on the Hebrew of the Old Testament and the Greek of the New Testament. The resolution for the new Bible read:

> That a translation be made of the whole Bible, as consonant
> as can be to the original Hebrew and Greek; and this to be
> set out and printed, without any marginal notes, and only
> to be used in all Churches in England in time of divine
> services.[142]

In 1607, forty-seven of the finest Greek and Hebrew scholars that could be found began work on this monumental task. The new version, which came to be known as the King James Version, was published in 1611. While it did not win immediate acceptance among the people, in time it became the accepted English translation. Even today, after 400 years, the King James Version is still the preference of many English speaking people.

Today there are a myriad of English translations. For over a thousand years ecclesiastical powers, as well as political powers, had sought to keep locked-up the Word of God, but, again, the Word of God cannot be bound. Try as man may to destroy the Bible, its indestructible nature will always outlast its political and ecclesiastical enemies.

Philosophical Opposition

As if political/governmental and ecclesiastical opposition are not enough, another hostile enemy the Bible faces is philosophical opposition. Unlike the political and ecclesiastical powers that sought to either physically destroy the Bible or keep it hidden away from the populace, philosophical opposition seeks to discredit the Bible as to its trustworthiness and reliability.

Philosophical opposition can be divided into two camps: agnostic and atheistic opposition that seeks to dismiss the Bible as untrue, and the liberal theologian who seeks to discredit and dismantle the Bible.

As the Christian faith began to spread, it didn't take long for someone to attack, in writing, the veracity of the Christian faith and Jesus. Considered to be the first written attacks upon the Christian faith, a work was composed in the second-century entitled, *True Discourse* or *True Word* written by Celsus about 178.[143] In his philosophical attack on Christianity, he disparagingly wrote about the virgin birth, the life of Jesus, his death, burial, and resurrection, and the writings of the Apostles. He saw the Christian faith as unreasonable, and when compared to Greek philosophies was woefully lacking. The words of Celsus are known by very, very few, but the indestructible Word of God has been proclaimed around the world.

In the third century, Porphyry (ca. 232–303) wrote several works attacking Christianity and the Scriptures. He was hostile toward the Christian faith, claiming Christians were a confused and dangerous sect. Only portions and fragments of his writings remain, but the Word of God abides forever!

Regardless of the century, or the era in which the skeptic lived, their attack is always the same; attacking the person of Christ and trustworthiness of Scripture. There are many representative voices that one could give ear too, but their venomous words eventually grow silent while the Word of God continues to speak

In chapter one, the views of Scottish David Hume (1711-1776) were examined. There will not be a revisiting of what was written earlier, other than to say Hume saw the Christian faith as born out of ignorance, superstition, and the Scriptures, which speak of miracles, are filled with mythology and folklore. The writings of Hume are read by few, but the Word of God is read by millions daily.

In France, the poisonous pen of Voltaire (1694-1778) attacked the Christian faith and the Bible like few ever have. He contended the Bible was full of errors and contradictions. He made fun of many of the stories that were in the Old Testament, believing they were primitive and fables. In his arrogance, he thought he "had overthrew the Bible . . . [and] entirely demolished the whole thing."[144] Voltaire predicted in 1776, "In less than a hundred years Christianity will have been swept from existence and will have passed into history."[145]

Voltaire died in 1778, and while his words have all but passed away, the Word of God shall never pass away. Interestingly, he had predicted that the Bible would eventually become a forgotten book, yet only fifty years after his death the very house from which he penned such words was purchased by the Geneva Bible Society as a place to store Bibles, and the printing press on which he had printed his blasphemous works was used to print Bibles![146]

In chapter one there was an examination of atheists German Fredrick Nietzsche and American Thomas Paine regarding their view of the Christian faith. Their blasphemous words against Christianity and the Bible will not be revisited here, but let it be said that while they have long since passed into history the Bible is still with us. Their words and pens did not move an inch the eternal anvil of God's Word.

In the last half of the nineteenth-century the voice of Robert Ingersoll (1833-1899) made a foolish prediction like that of Voltaire. Because of his eloquent oratory skills he drew large crowds where ever he went. Influenced by the writings of Voltaire and Paine, he traveled far and wide speaking against Christianity and the Bible. In the 1890's Ingersoll made a prediction about the Bible, "In fifteen years I will have this Book in the morgue."[147] In fifteen years it was not the Bible that was in the morgue, but it was Ingersoll, who suddenly died in 1899. He, too, beat upon the eternal anvil of God's Word and made not a dent in it.

Sidney Collett sums up the foolish boasts of men like Voltaire and Ingersoll, and all like them, "We might as well put our shoulder to the burning wheel of the sun, and try to stop it on its flaming course, as attempt to stop the circulation of the Bible."[148]

In addition to those in the philosophical camp who are openly antagonist to the Word of God and seek to rid the earth of the Bible, there are those who are theologically liberal who seek to discredit it.

With the dawning of what has been labeled the Enlightenment or the Age of Reason, philosophical thought was elevated to the place of the deification of human logic and reason. The motto of the Enlightenment period is best summarized by Immanuel Kant (1724-1804) who wrote, "Enlightenment is man's release from his self-incurred tutelage. Tutelage is man's inability to make use of his understanding without direction from another . . . Dare to know. Have courage to use your own reason—that is the motto of the enlightenment"[149]

The movement was watered by such philosophical thinkers as Descartes (1596-1650), Spinoza (1632-1677), and Leibniz (1646-1716), and Kant. Reason became the test tube of life through which all things must pass. All of life was put under the microscope of reason and the ability of man by human reason to know truth. Apologist Norman Geisler writes, "Basically, rationalists hold that what is knowable or demonstratable by human reason is true."[150] In other words, that which is above the reach of reason or cannot be attained by reason is unreasonable and unknowable.

The starting point in rationalism is not God, but human reason. As Descartes stated, "I think, therefore I am." The only thing man can be certain of is the existence of himself because he is a thinking being, it is from this starting point man seeks to know truth. According to Descartes one "must avoid believing things which are not entirely certain and indubitable."[151]

James Livingston says of the Enlightenment or Age of Reason, "The ideal of the Enlightenment is the duty of not entertaining any belief that is not warranted by rational evidence, which means by the assent of autonomous reason rather than biblical or ecclesiastical authority."[152]

Philosophical rationalism became the seeds for theological liberalism which approaches the Bible with a critical approach. Spinoza (1632-1677) was one of the first to subject the Bible to the microscope of reason. In his work, *Theologico Political Tractatus* (1670), he critically analyzed the religion of the Bible contending that it must be subjected to critical reasoning.[153] He rejected miracles, prophecy, and the supernatural because it goes against the nature of reason. As the result of Spinoza's work, he has been called the father of "higher criticism."

Higher Criticism become associated with the liberal camp, which approaches the biblical text based primarily on skepticism, rationalistic and naturalistic assumptions rather than revelation or faith. Its method of interpretation became destructive not constructive. Higher Criticism has, in large measure, been used it as a tool to discredit the inspiration of the Bible, relegating it to only a human book that is full of errors and inaccuracies.

The influence of Spinoza, and those who ascribed to his philosophical thought, had far reaching effects, as others begin to approach the Bible with the same critical reasoning. Spilling over into the theological arena, the "higher criticism" approach to the Bible found a home in the mid-nineteenth century in Germany in the Tubingen School of F.C Baur (1792-1860).

The approach of the Tubingen School to the Bible was one of rationalistic skepticism. Miracles were denied, the supernatural questioned, the authorship of the books doubted, the deity of Jesus denied, and inspiration of Scripture tossed aside. The Bible was seen as a mere human book. The radical anti-supernaturalism approach to biblical interpretation became the trademark of the Tubingen School. The presuppositions which those of this camp brought to the Bible were destructive, and they denied the very foundation of the Christian faith.

Conservative theologians, led by Ernst Hengstenberg (1802-1869), opposed the methodology of Tubingen School and sought to refute their conclusions. With the death of Baur in 1860, the Tubingen School lost the importance and influence it once had. The writings of those who once approached the Bible with an anti-supernatural bias now gather dust.

There have been those liberal theologians since, like Rudolf Bultmann (1884-1976), and his demythologization (removing the myths) of the twentieth-century, who have sought to take up the mantel of the methodology of the Tubingen School and strip the Bible of its trustworthiness.

Currently, the skeptical pen of Bart Ehrman, religion professor at UNC-Chapel Hill, seeks through his writings to discredit the trustworthiness and reliability of the Bible.[154] His most current book is entitled, *Forged: Writing in the Name of God: Why the Bible's Authors Are Not Who We Think They Are*. About the biblical writers he states, "The authors intended to deceive their readers, and their readers were all too easily deceived. The use of deception to promote the truth may well be considered one of the most unsettling ironies of the early Christian tradition."[155]

Such a statement implies that all Christ said and did was a lie and the entire Bible is a lie, and every follower of Christ who has ever lived has been deceived by a lie. Ehrman would have one believe the Bible and Christianity is all a big hoax.

When it comes to deception, the ones deceived are those who arrogantly raise their voices to attack the indestructible Word of God.

Like all who have gone before him, Ehrman's efforts to discredit the Bible will prove futile. The day will come when the pen of all who have and do seek to write disparagingly of the Bible, will write no more. There will only be one book left standing, still unscathed by all attackers. That book is the Bible.

Those who would attack the creditability of the Bible have marched across the stage of life and raised their voices against it. Their voices in time are silenced, rendering the circulation of their works to only a handful. The Bible, though, with its indestructible quality, weathers all attacks from the opposition and continues worldwide circulation.

It matters not where the attacks have come from, whether it has been political/governmental attacks, ecclesiastical attacks, or attacks from philosophy and liberal theologians, the Bible has withstood them all. It is the most widely circulated and read book in the world. Attackers still beat upon this Eternal Anvil, but in the end it always proves indestructible. The Bible time and time again, has proved itself to be more than a book of man's wisdom, but a Book that is divinely inspired by God.

H.L. Hastings wrote in 1890 words that still echo with eternal truth today even though over one hundred years have passed:

> Infidels for eighteen hundred years have been refuting and overthrowing this book, and yet it stands today as solid as a rock. Its circulation increases, and it is more loved and cherished and read today than ever before. Infidels, with all their assaults, make about as much impression on this book as a man with a tack hammer would on the Pyramids of Egypt. When the French monarch proposed the persecution of the Christians in his dominion, an old statesman and warrior said to him, "Sire, the church of God is an anvil that has worn out many hammers." So the hammers of infidels have been pecking away at this book for ages, but the hammers are worn out, and the anvil still endures. If this book had not been the book of God, men would have destroyed it long ago. Emperors and popes,

kings and priests, princes and rulers have tried their hand at it; they die and the book still lives.[156]

The Bible's indestructibility is truly a compelling argument for the truthfulness of the Old Book being the divinely inspired word of God.

CHAPTER 9
PRACTICALITY FOR LIVING AFFIRMS BIBLE'S INSPIRATION

In an age of moral and ethical relativism, when codes of conduct are about as plenteous as stars in the sky, are there moral and ethical standards which transcend what man can produce? Is there a universal standard of morality that exists to undergird the core of man's being as it relates to him and others? Is man left to himself to engineer his own values and morality, or are there any eternal principles that will serve to benefit him regardless of ethnicity, geographical location, or the era in which he lives?

There are those who contend that each individual is left to themselves to form their own value system of what is right and wrong. To adopt such a philosophy implies that what is right for one might not be right for another; and what is wrong for one may not be wrong for another. Since there is no eternal or universal ethical and moral standard we can all mold our own personal value system.

In embracing the Bible as the divinely inspired Word of God, it only stands to reason that the Creator who has chosen to reveal Himself in history and record the unfolding of His purpose to redeem man, that He would not leave him without an eternal standard of what is morally and ethically right. The God who took the initiative to reveal Himself to man, has also taken the initiative to reveal to him principles that are practical for conducting his life.

The sixth compelling truth for the Bible being the divinely inspired Word of God is its practicality for living. The non-complexity and practicality of the Bible's moral system surpasses the ever changing moral systems of man. Its enduring and eternal quality affirms a divine Mind behind its creation.

In chapter four, when the thematic unity of the Bible was examined, there was an examination of the moral and ethical unity that is interwoven throughout the whole of the Bible. A revisiting of some of the material previously covered is necessary in order to adequately expand upon the practicality of biblical morality.

From the beginning of God's revelation to humanity He let it be known the He was superior to the tribal gods created by man's wisdom and hands. From the early chapters of Genesis one discovers a God who is holy, moral, and ethical in His character. He is a God who has set standards and parameters for man's behavior in regard to himself and to his fellowman.

The God who created Adam and Eve set moral and ethical standards that were for their good and their best. When they stepped outside those moral boundaries, it created consequences that affected them and all who would descend from them (Romans 5:12).

When Abraham was called by God, he separated himself from the pagan atmosphere of those around him who worshipped many gods, to follow the one true God who demanded a different lifestyle (Genesis 12). The polytheistic gods Abraham was familiar with had no ethical or moral parameters, as followers of such gods lived without restraints.

The Canaanites, with their vile and immoral religious practices, were a constant threat to the moral atmosphere of the Jews. The Canaanite system of worship was morally depraved, as its participants sacrificed their children in the fire to Moloch, practiced homosexuality, and bestiality (Leviticus 18:21-23). Their moral behavior was so vile that it resulted in the Lord warning the Hebrews to have no dealings with them and refrain from becoming involved in their debased practices. The Jews were commanded by God not to go after "the doings of the land of Canaan, where I am bringing you, you shall not do; nor shall you walk in their ordinances" (Leviticus 18:3).

God's people were expected to live by a higher standard of morality, and keep His statues and judgments and "walk in them" (Leviticus 18:4-5). Such moral and ethical behavior was foreign in the religious practices of surrounding tribes and nations. The Lord God of the Bible revealed Himself as One who demanded exemplary conduct that respected others and upheld the integrity of the individual.

Though Noah, Abraham, Isaac, and Jacob experienced their own sins and failures, the Lord called them to strive to live by a higher moral code than others around them. Their ethical behavior was to be anchored in their relationship with the true God.

When Moses received the Ten Commandments (Exodus 20), God gave the Jews a moral foundation that has been a rock on which down through the centuries has been sufficient for individuals, and nations, to build upon. Critics contend that Moses could not have written the Ten Commandments at the time the Bible says he received them because they are too advanced for his time. That, however, is just the point. It was God who gave Moses those commandants which were advanced for that day and time. Where else would Moses have gotten such an advanced moral system if not from God?

A look at the Ten Commandments reveals how advanced they were for that day and time. The commandments emphasize, first, man's relationship with God, and, second, man's relationship with others. The Ten Commandments are found in Exodus 20:1-12, and Deuteronomy 5:1-22. While originally given to the Jews, they are timeless moral principles that have stood the test of time and relevant for any life and any society.

First, the Jews were commanded, "You shall have no other gods before Me" (Exodus 20:2-3). God delivered them from the bondage of Egypt, and out of gratitude they were to worship Him and Him alone. In a day when their neighbors were polytheistic, the Jews were monotheistic, worshiping only the one true God.

Second, the Jews were not to make a graven image of any kind to bow down and worship (Exodus 20:4-7). God is a Spirit who must be worshipped in spirit and truth (John 4:23-24), unlike the polytheistic gods whose images were worshipped in idolatry.

Third, the Jews were not to take the name of the Lord in vain (Exodus 20:7). The name of God was to be reverenced and not used in a contemptuous manner. To use the name of God in such a way is a show of disrespect. The Jews were to honor God's name with consistency in the words they spoke and in the way they lived.

Fourth, the Jews were to remember the Sabbath (Exodus 20:8-11). Genesis chapters one and two record God's creation of the world, and all that was in it in six days. The Jews were to rest on the Sabbath, the seventh day, and remember the Creator in worship. In keeping the Sabbath man replenished his body in rest from work and replenished his soul through worship of God.

Fifth, the Jews were to honor their father and mother (Exodus 20:12). Parents were/are to be honored for giving the individual life, for providing for the needs of their children, and for their wisdom in seeking to lead their children aright. As father and mother age, the child is to remember their parents looked after them when they were unable to look after themselves, therefore; children are to return the love and care.

Sixth, the Jews were forbidden to murder (Exodus 20:13). The Jews were to respect life and not in cold-blood spill innocent blood. Every human being is created in the image of God, and to shed innocent blood is a sin against the sanctity of life and the God who created that individual in His image.

Seventh, the Jews were not to commit adultery (Exodus 20:14). Marriage is a sacred bond ordained by God between a man and a woman (Genesis 2:24), and a sexual relationship between someone other than one's spouse is an affront to the marriage relationship. When one steps outside the marriage bond it damages and brings sorrow to all involved. It is God who ordained monogamous relationships. Monogamy was truly out of character in the culture of that day.

Eighth, the Jews were not to steal (Exodus 20:15). Another person's property and what they own is to be respected. Without this respect for what belongs to others it would bring chaos to society. The individual is to be honest and a person of integrity. If one desires anything, they are encouraged to work for it and not take it from someone else.

Ninth, the Jews were not to bear false witness against someone (Exodus 20:16). No one is to destroy another individual's reputation by speaking falsely against them. To steal someone's good name by false accusations is a form of robbery and murder.

Tenth, the Jews were not to covet their neighbor's wife or anything else that did not belong to them (Exodus 20:17). Covetousness is an attitude, which if not held in check, can create a dislike for another individual who has something others do not have. Covetousness is another kind of idolatry (Ephesians 5:5).

The Ten Commandants set a high standard for the Jews that were unprecedented for that day. Recognizing the superiority of what Moses presented to them, the people raised their voices as one in agreement to abide by what would separate them from their neighbor in regard to behavior and conduct (Exodus 24:3)

Now the critic is quick to point out that the Jews on many occasions failed to live up to the moral and ethical standards that were revealed to them. Throughout the Old Testament we find the Jews from time to time becoming involved in pagan worship though forbidden to do so, having more than one wife, brutalizing their fellowman, bearing false witness, shedding innocent blood, disrespecting the sanctity of life, and taking from others what was not theirs.

Such accusations are true, the Jews did not always live up to the moral and ethical precepts they had been given. There were times when it was hard to distinguish between them and their heathen neighbors in regard to their conduct. However, even though the Jews did not always live up to the high standard which the Lord had revealed to them, that does not annul the fact that the moral and ethical teachings were superior and advanced for that day and time.

The fact the Jews disobeyed the Lord never revoked His command that they were to follow His precepts. Prophet after prophet came on the scene who continually would admonish the people to live what had been revealed to them.

Disobedience did not and does not remove the moral boundaries God sets for humanity. The negative consequences of disobedience, as the Jews discovered every time they disobeyed, reminds one of the necessity of moral and ethical boundaries for the individual and society. Every time the Jews abandoned the Lord's high standards for how they should live they found themselves being oppressed by a foreign power (book of Judges), and eventually going into captivity. Their attempting to change the parameters of what was right and wrong, always revealed that those parameters cannot be changed and there are disastrous consequences when one tries to do so.

When the Jews were disobedient it actually affirmed the superiority of the moral precepts that the Lord had revealed to them, as they realized the ways of the heathen does not work. They would then be drawn back to the precepts the Lord had entrusted to them. Even in their sometimes disobedience God never relinquished His call to them to live by higher standards than their neighbors, nor did He ever abandon His purpose through them to bring about His ultimate purpose, which was the redemption of humanity.

Peter Craigie writes in his excellent book, *The Problem of War in the Old Testament,* of this paradox of God continually working through the Jews even though they did not always live up to the high standards committed unto them:

> In order to achieve the ultimate redemption of man, God acts through human beings. He acts in the world as it is, for if the prerequisite for divine action were sinless men and sinless societies, God could not act through human beings and human institutions at all . . . That the Jews often failed is not a reflection on God, but on the nation of Israel; it is a reflection on mankind. [Our] hope is for the presence and participation of God in our own evil world, a world which might seem by definition to exclude even the possibility of knowing and experiencing God.[157]

God, by the revelation of Himself, has chosen to participate in this world, and in so doing gives moral precepts of how those He created should live. Even though the Jews at times did not live as they should, the moral and ethical foundation found in the Ten Commandments has never been abolished. It is the foundation of the Judeo-Christian ethic.

Interestingly, the moral and ethical precepts found in the Ten Commandments have been through the centuries a foundation for the laws of every civilized country, nation, and state. Their timeless practicality provides a standard for stability and order to societies and individuals who incorporate them into their public laws and individual lives.

Years ago this writer was talking to a man about his relationship with the Lord. The man replied that he did not believe in God, but that he did believe in the moral teachings found in the Bible. He said he believed that if one sought to live their life according to the Ten Commandments, the Sermon on the Mount, and the teachings of Jesus then one's life would turn out well for them and their fellowman. In essence, this man was saying the Bible's moral and ethical teachings are practical and applicable to a person's life even if they didn't believe in the God of the Bible.

Over the years this writer has heard other skeptics echo the same words, which attest to the Bible's practicality for living. Wherever the moral and ethical precepts of this Book have held sway there has been a beneficial influence. Augustus H. Strong writes, "The perfection of this [moral] system is generally conceded. All will admit that it greatly surpasses any other system known among men."[158]

One of the leading Founding Fathers of America, Thomas Jefferson (1743-1826), contended the ethical teachings of Jesus, as found in the Gospels, were superior to any other teachings found in the world. Taking from the Bible the moral and ethical teachings of Jesus, he even had published a work entitled, *The Life and Morals of Jesus of Nazareth Extracted Textually from the Gospels* (c 1820).[159] While he sought to separate the religious elements from His moral teachings, Jefferson recognized that the infant United States could not prosper if it did not adopt a moral and ethical code that would respect the dignity of each individual. He found that moral code in the Bible.

Jefferson stated, "Of all the systems of morality, ancient or modern, which come under my observation, none appear to me so pure as that of Jesus . . . The studious perusal of the sacred volume will make better citizens, better fathers, and better husbands."[160]

The nation's first President, George Washington, echoed Jefferson's sentiments. He said, "It is impossible to govern rightly the world without God and the Bible.[161]

By examining the practical principles of the Bible one can readily see its moral superiority over other moral systems, whether they be some philosophical system or another religion. The principles found in the Bible speak to all the practical areas of human life. The Ten Commandments are the foundation from which all other moral and ethical principles flow.

The Bible spends much time giving practical instructions on how one should conduct their lives and treat their fellow man. A look at the teachings found just in the book of Proverbs reveals the practicality of its wisdom. When one reads through Proverbs there is found practical advice for every area of one's life. A few examples are cited with selected verses regarding the practicality of Proverbs as it deals with the living of life.

Proverbs addresses the subject of adultery (5:1-23; 6:20-35; 7:1-27); the dangers of the abuse of alcohol (20:1; 21:17; 23:29-35; 31:4-7); the need to control one's anger (6:34; 14:17; 14:29; 16:32; 29:8; 29:22); avoid bribery (17:8; 17:23; 21:14; 29:4); advice not to be deceitful (10:10; 12:5; 12:20; 16:30; 27:6); discipline of children (3:11-12; 13:1; 13:24; 15:5; 22:6); avoiding evil (2:10-15; 3:7; 3:29-30; 6:16-19; 17:13; 27:12); fearing the Lord (1:7; 1:28-29; 2:1-5; 15:33 19:13); matters pertaining to food (12:11; 20:13; 10:17; 22:9; 23:6-8; 28:19); do not be a fool (1:7; 10:10; 11:29; 17:12; 17:28; 18:6-7); relationships with friends and neighbors (3:27-29); 6:1-3; 6:27-29; 19:6;27:17); on giving (3:27-28; 14:31; 18:16; 19:17); warning against greed (11:6; 11:26; 27:20); on seeking guidance (3:5-6; 11:3; 11:14; 24:5-60); on the home (11:29; 14:1; 15:6; 15:25; 24:3-4); on honesty (11:1; 16:11; 20:10; 20:23; 25:19); living honorably (3:35; 10:7; 20:29; 22:4; 29:23); doing justly (8:15; 18:5; 21:3; 28:21); on being kind to others (3:3-4; 11:17; 14:22; 19:22); obtaining knowledge (1:7; 2:10; 9:10; 10:14); laziness (10:4-5; 12:24; 12:27;13:4; 20:13); on love (8:20-21; 10:12; 15:17; 16:13; 17:17); lying (6:16-19; 10:18; 12:19; 12:22); advice to parents (1:8-9; 4:1-6; 20:7; 22:6); advice to political leaders (8:14-16; 14:28; 14:34-35; 16:12-15; 20:18; 29:4); advice on treatment of poor (3:34; 14:31; 19:17; 21:13); on prayer (15:8; 15:29; 28:13); advice against pride (8:13; 11:2; 15:25; 28:25; 29:23); on living righteous (2:7; 9:9; 11:30; 20:7; 10:6-7); advice to scoffers (1:22; 3:34; 9:12; 14:9); using self-control (14:17; 15:18; 17:14; 29:11); using sound speech (4:24; 6:12; 10:11; 12:18); advice about lending money (6:1-5; 11:15; 17:18; 22:26-

27); on obtaining truth (3:3-4; 12:17; 20:28; 23:23); don't engage in violence (1:10-19; 3:3032;24:1-2;29:10); proper use of wealth (3:9-10; 3:13-16;10:20; 11:28); against the wicked (10:27; 17:19; 24:19-20); seeking wisdom (1:20-33; 2:1-12;4:3-9); advice to women (14:1; 18:22; 30:20; 31:10-31), obeying the Word of God (2:6; 13:13; 16:20); and admonishment to work (10:4; 14:23; 16:26; 28:19).

More areas of everyday living could be cited with accompanying verses, but the examples cited are enough to affirm that just in Proverbs alone there are moral and ethical precepts that deal with the practical areas of one's life.

God's emphasis on high moral and ethical behavior is seen all through the Bible. There is not a book in the Bible where some moral or ethical topic is not mentioned and addressed. If one doubts the benefits of applying the precepts and principles of the Bible to their lives, a reading of Psalm 119 reveals the many benefits for those who walk in moral and ethical integrity. To love His precepts and walk in them is to live a life blessed by the Creator (Psalm 119:1-2).

When one reads the prophets it will be found that they all echo Micah's declaration when describing the walk of a moral and ethical person, "He has shown you, O man, what is good; and what does the Lord require of you, but to do justly, and to love mercy, and to walk humbly with your God?" (Micah 6:8, KJV).

In the New Testament we find Jesus in the Sermon of the Mount (Matthew 5-7) teaching on the moral and ethical conduct of a Kingdom citizen. Living by the Golden Rule was admonished, "Therefore, whatever you want men to do to you, do also to them, for this is the Law and the Prophets" (Matt.7:12).

Jesus even elevated the moral behavior taught in the Old Testament, addressing more than one's conduct but the attitude and thinking that forms one's behavior (Matthew 5:21-48). For instance, Jesus took the commandment that forbade adultery and spoke of the lustful thoughts that leads to the act itself (Matthew 5:27-28). Taking the commandment to respect human life and murder, he addressed the emotion of anger that preceded the act. Jesus not only endorsed the moral laws of God, he raised the bar for Kingdom citizens to live radically different.

All the apostles, Paul, Peter, John and James, all admonish the Christian to walk worthy in the Lord (Ephesians 4:1), to abstain from immorality (I Thessalonians 4:3), do not lie (Ephesians 4:25), do not steal (Ephesians 4:28), do not be prideful but be humble (James 4:6), do not be covetousness (James 5:1-3), do not gossip, (2 Thessalonians 3:11), do not let bitterness overtake you (Ephesians 4:31), if you do not work you do not eat (2 Thessalonians 3:12), avoid selfishness and speaking evil of others (James 4:11), and be attentive to give loving treatment to one's spouse (Ephesians 5:5:22-30).

When reading Revelation, the last book in the Bible, the followers of Christ are encouraged, even in times of persecution, to continue to live a life of moral and ethical integrity of "works, love, service, faith, and patience" (Rev. 2:19).

One can search other religions and other philosophical systems, but one will not find when it comes to moral and ethical teachings the comprehensives as found in the Bible. While strains of moral and ethical truths can be found in other writings and other religions, they are simply echoing what has already been declared in the Bible. Joseph Cook has stated, "Jewels there are in the teaching of other men, but they are jewels picked out of the mud."

John Adams (1735-1826), a signer of the Declaration of Independence and the nation's second President, wrote concerning the Bible's moral superiority, "The Christian religion is, above all the religions that ever prevailed or existed in ancient or modern times, the religion of wisdom, virtue, equity and humanity."[162]

R.A. Torrey in the early part of the twentieth century wrote, "It is quite fashionable in some quarters to compare the teaching of the Bible with the teachings of Zoroaster and Buddha and Confucius and Epictetus and Socrates and Marcus Aurelius, Antonius and a number of other heathen authors."[163] Torrey went on to affirm the superiority of the Bible, saying, "Put all these truths that you have culled from the literature of all ages into one book, and as the result, even then you will not have a book that will take the place of this one Book."[164]

There may be grains of moral and ethical truths found in the writings of Pythagoras, Socrates, Plato, Aristotle, Epicurus, Zeno, and many philosophers who followed them, but whatever truths they have gleaned from life are already found in the Bible. The same is true of the many religions of the world. They, as well, may contain strains of moral truth, but they only echo what truths are already found in Scripture.

In the twenty-first century there needs to be a return to the timeless, practical precepts found in the Word of God. The principles found in the Bible were not just for those of ancient times, but they will work and are applicable for the technological world lived in today, as matter a fact they are a must.

Regardless of how knowledgeable an individual or a nation may be, without moral standards to guide man there is always degeneration in his behavior and in his treatment of his fellowman. History has born this out in the decline of nations like Israel and in the Roman Empire. Both nations, the citizens within those nations, lived without restraint, ignoring the practical moral principles that God gave to humanity regarding how one should conduct their lives. As a result the nations eventually collapsed inwardly.

The United States was built on the timeless principles of the Bible. Daniel Webster (1782-1852), an early American statesman, said, "Our ancestors established their system of government on morality and [biblical] sentiment. Moral habits, they believed, cannot safely be trusted on any other foundation than religious principle, nor any government be secure which is not supported by moral habits."[165]

There has been a drifting, however, a shifting in the foundation on which this nation was built. Can anyone deny a shifting of the nation's moral foundation? People today have lost their moral compass and when this happens, when there is an ignoring of biblical moral and ethical precepts, a downward spiral into chaos and confusion occurs.

The Bible teaches the fundamental truth of the sanctity of human life and man is to respect that sacredness. Since it was God who created man and breathed into him the breath of life (Genesis 2:7), each person is to treat the other person with recognition of this human valuablness. Where this principle has been followed societies have been orderly and prospered. History has borne out that where this principle has been neglected oppression and tyranny have resulted.

Society today has forsaken the truth of the sanctity and sacredness of life as a fundamental and cherished principle, and as a result abortion has become a tolerated and an accepted practice. Recognizing life is created by God is what gives dignity to man, and affirms the sanctity of life. Whenever there is a regression from the Light given to man there is a departure from this sacred principle (Romans 1:19-23), and life is devalued.

The principle of the sacredness of marriage between a man and woman is being attacked today as being no longer applicable for the twenty-first century, and should no longer be the only accepted family unit. As a result of this attack on family values we see the continual push to accept and make law same sex marriages.

The principle of honesty has been tossed aside, as individuals like Bernie Madoff, who cheated clients out of billions of dollars, are becoming more and more prevalent. Greed has replaced integrity as a bedrock principle in dealing with others. The Golden Rule of doing unto others what one would desire should be done unto them, has been replaced with the principle of taking from others before they take it from you.

The principle of working hard to achieve success in life has been replaced with an entitlement mentality like that of the Prodigal Son (Luke 15), and a "you owe me" attitude prevails regardless of whether or not one deserves it or worked for it.

Living beyond one's means and abandoning restraint in regard to monetary matters has plunged individuals and this nation into unsustainable debt. Ignoring biblical principles dealing with greed and covetousness are at the root of the problem, as well as mismanagement.

The ills that plague society today are the result of abandoning the timeless moral and ethical principles of the Word of God. There is a practicality in the principles of God's Word. When they are applied to everyday life one finds they work, when one ignores them they work against them.

The moral slide seen in society and the chaos that results from such a slide can be stopped when individuals return to the simple and practical precepts found in the Bible. Noah Webster (1758-1843), father of the American dictionary, writes regarding the necessity for individuals to continually live by the biblical moral code:

The moral principles and precepts contained in the Scriptures ought to form the basis of all our civil constitutions and laws. All the miseries and evils which men suffer from vice, crime, ambition, injustice, oppression, slavery, and war, proceed from their despising or neglecting the precepts contained in the Bible.[166]

Moral slides, however, begin when the God who gave us moral and ethical principles by which to live is forsaken, resulting in man seeking to devise his own moral system that is always inferior to the morality of the Bible. Departure from the practical moral and ethical principles of the Bible is a venture that history has shown will fail every time. History has shown that when individuals within a society abandon the biblical moral system it eventually, as Strong says, "Reduces men to a dead level of social depression, despotism, and semi–barbarism."[167]

The Bible's practical precepts are anchored in a God who created man and how He has given him principles to live by that elevate the sacredness and dignity of man. Man's reliance must be on the One who created him in order to be enabled to live up to those high standards.

As has been seen, the God who created man has not left him here to devise his own existential value system, but has provided for those He created practical precepts that have stood the test of time. Ethicist Paul Simmons writes, "Scripture is regarded as an indispensable guide to the faith and practice of the [Christian] . . . The Bible offers specific moral directives that are foundational for all Christian moral thought."[168] It is a foundation that transcends any value system man attempts to build.

Strong writes:

The beneficent influence of the Scripture doctrines and precepts, wherever they have had sway, shows their divine origin . . . We may justly argue that a moral system so pure and perfect, since it surpasses all human powers of invention and runs counter to men's natural tastes and passions, must have had a supernatural, and if a supernatural, then a divine origin. [169]

Regardless of man's continued attempt to change the boundaries of what is right and wrong, the moral and ethical teachings of Scripture have weathered the test of time and have been a light that neither time nor culture can extinguish. It is a supernatural light that transcends time and culture because its source originates in the eternal character of a holy God.

The Bible's practicality for living is a compelling argument for the truthfulness of it being the divinely inspired Word of God.

CHAPTER 10
MORAL LIFE OF JESUS AFFIRMS BIBLE'S INSPIRATION

Few would deny that Jesus is the most famous, and, as well, the most controversial figure in history. All humanity is confronted with a decision regarding His life, His claims, and His teachings. Jesus asked His disciples a personal question, "But who do you say that I am?" (Matthew 16:15). That is a question each person must answer. Will He be accepted as a mere man, or One who is both human and divine? Was He truthful in all that He said, or did He deliberately deceive in some of the words He spoke? Can His life be considered one of moral excellence if He intentionally lied?

In the last chapter, the Bible's practicality for living was examined, which also encompasses the life and teachings of Jesus, presenting as a compelling argument for the Bible as being divinely inspired. While not all accept the divinity of Jesus, many see the moral life He exemplified, and the moral teachings He expounded, worthy of following and emulating. Jesus is seen as a moral philosopher, and the principles He taught and exhibited in His life are valuable for all humanity to incorporate into their lives.

It is the contention of this writer, that the Bible is the divinely inspired Word of God, meaning that what it says about the divinity of Jesus is true. However, many who are non-Christians, while not acknowledging the divinity of Jesus, hail the moral life and teachings of Jesus worthy of following. Such a confession and affirmation regarding the moral excellence of the life of Jesus is a seventh compelling truth for the Bible as being divinely inspired.

Many non-Christians contend the moral teachings of Jesus transcend religion, even whether one believes in God or not. Jesus taught, among many moral truths, each was to love their neighbor, to be honest, to be compassionate and caring, treat others as you would like to be treated, help the poor and unfortunate, forgive those who wrong us, and to keep our word in dealing with others. How could such moral teachings not be embraced?

As a moral system for human behavior and conduct, the teachings of Jesus are shining stars in a dark world. But can the moral teachings of Jesus be separated from what He said about Himself without destroying His moral excellence? Before answering that question, a look at what non-believers, and even liberal Christians, have said about the moral life and teachings of Jesus will prove enlightening.

The following quotes from the mouths of some who don't necessarily label themselves as Christian, affirm Jesus as being a great moral teacher, whose principles can impact and bring stability to one's life and to society.

Josephus, the first century Jewish historian, acknowledged the superiority of the wisdom and teachings of Jesus, and the impact they had on many who came under His influence. He writes in *Antiquities*, "About this time there lived Jesus, a wise man, if indeed one should call him a man. For he was a performer of astonishing deeds, a teacher of men who are happy to accept the truth. He won over many Jews and indeed also many Greeks . . . And still to this day the tribe of Christians, named after him, has not disappeared."[170]

Concerning the life of Jesus, Thomas Paine's skeptical pen wrote in the *Age of Reason*, "[Jesus Christ] was a virtuous and an amiable man. The morality that he preached and practiced was of the most benevolent kind; and though similar systems of morality had been preached by . . . . many good men in all ages, it has not been exceeded by any."

Once talking to a non-believer, while dismissing the divinity of Jesus, affirmed the soundness of His moral teachings, saying, "Though Jesus was an important moral philosopher, there is no proof He was divine."

Mike Magee, while rejecting salvation by faith, adheres to the moral teachings of Jesus as the way of salvation. He writes in, *What Matters Most, Christ's Resurrection or His Moral Teaching?*

> Christians have abandoned Christ's moral teaching for Paul's mystical teaching [of salvation by faith]. As a consequence morality has been lost while selfishness has burgeoned. Morality is concern for others. Faith is concern for self. Christ taught salvation is earned by service to others . . . Instead of quoting Paul's magical and mysterious statements, Christians should get into the habit of quoting Christ's very plain and understandable principles of personal morality.[171]

Fannie B. James, co-founder of Divine Science (1877), which seeks divine oneness with God, believed the teachings of Jesus would lead a person to salvation by opening their understanding. She wrote that Jesus was the Universal Man, and she defined salvation as, "A return to true consciousness that destroys all false conceptions of life. Being saved from erroneous opinions and beliefs. Understanding is the only salvation and Jesus' whole life was spent in opening man's thought to understanding. He said the truth [His teachings] shall make you free."[172] Though Divine Science believes in a universal "source," the moral example and principles of Jesus are to be highly esteemed.

Fyodor Dostoyevsky (1821-1881), an existentialist, wrote, "Even those who have renounced Christianity and attack it, in their inmost being still follow the Christian ideal, for hitherto neither their subtlety nor the ardor of their hearts has been able to create a higher ideal of man and of virtue than the ideal given by Christ of old."[173]

Larry Chapman, editor of *Y-Jesus Magazine*, writes:

> Almost all scholars acknowledge that Jesus was a great moral teacher. In fact, his brilliant insight into human morality is an accomplishment recognized even by those of other religions. In his book *Jesus of Nazareth*, Jewish scholar Joseph Klausner wrote, "It is universally admitted . . . that

Christ taught the purest and sublimest ethics . . . which throws the moral precepts and maxims of the wisest men of antiquity far into the shade."[174]

In the last chapter, it was seen that Thomas Jefferson acknowledged the superiority of the teachings of Jesus over any other system of morality, ancient or modern.

Even the atheistic Nietzsche, as unrelenting as he was in his attacks on Christianity, recognized the uniqueness of the moral life of Jesus. He stated, "In reality there has been only one Christian, and he died on the Cross . . . The 'bringer of glad tidings' died as he had lived, as he had taught—not to 'redeem men' but to show how one must live."[175]

In the twelfth century, there was even developed what has been called the Moral Influence Theory of the atonement, which centered on the moral example of Jesus. Developed by Peter Abelard (1079-1142), those who hold to the Moral Influence Theory of the atonement believe that salvation is not obtained by the death of Christ on the cross as payment or satisfaction for sin, but rather Christ's death on the cross so impacts man that it inspires him to follow Christ and His teachings. In other words, Christ's love and His death is an example that spurs us to good works and service to our fellowman.

According to those who hold to the Moral Influence Theory, Christ did not die in order to pay for our sins, but instead He lived and died to serve as an example of love and mercy. His life and death remind us of how we need to live and how we must act in regards to our attitude and actions. Christ's example is supposed to be an influence on us rather than a ransom for us.

In response to the Moral Influence Theory of the atonement, Robert H. Culpeper, former professor at Southeastern Baptist Theological Seminary, writes:

It is in giving His Son to save us that God demonstrates His love. But in denying any objective element in the atonement and by ignoring the great body of scriptural teaching concerning Christ as the ransom for our sins and concerning His bearing our sins, the moral influence view [reverses] the order . . . The subjective [inward] appropriation of the atonement depends upon the objective fact of the atonement.[176]

While the Moral Influence Theory contradicts the teaching of the New Testament of the substitutionary death of Christ, and ultimately teaches a salvation by one's own works, it acknowledges the moral excellence of the life of Jesus.

Ernest Renan (1823-1892), philosopher and theologian, who ascribed to the historical criticism method of biblical interpretation, stated, "Jesus was the greatest religious genius that ever lived . . . Whatever may be the surprise of the future, [the teachings of] Jesus will never be surpassed."[177]

Richard Rothe (1799-1867), German theologian and ethicist, has written, "I know no other ground on which I could anchor my whole being, and particularly my speculations, except that historical phenomenon, Jesus Christ."[178]

Sholem Asch (1880-1957), a Jewish novelist and essayist, wrote, "No other teacher—Jewish, Christian, Buddhist, Mohammedan—is still a teacher whose teaching is such a guidepost for the world we live in . . . every act and word of Jesus has value for all of us."[179]

An unknown writer has written, "Socrates taught for 40 years, Plato for 50, Aristotle for 40, and Jesus for only 3. Yet the influence of Christ's teaching and three-year ministry infinitely transcends the impact left by the combined 130 years of teaching from these men who were among the greatest philosophers of all antiquity."

Christian apologist J.P. Moreland sums-up the many superlative statements about the moral life and teachings of Jesus, stating, "It has long been recognized that, irrespective of one's religious views about Jesus of Nazareth, He is one of the world's leading ethical thinkers and teachers." [180]

Interestingly, many who dismiss Jesus' claims in regard to what He had to say about the inspiration of Scripture and His claim to being the fulfillment of the prophesied Messiah, acknowledge the superiority of His life and moral teachings. However, can one claim Jesus was a great moral teacher or philosopher if it is believed He was untrue in

His statements about Himself being the Messiah and the Bible being inspired?

If the claim of Jesus to be divine is not true, then would not Jesus be a liar? Josh McDowell writes in *More Than a Carpenter*, "If, when Jesus made his claims, he knew that he was not God, then he was lying and deliberately deceiving his followers. But if he was a liar, then he was also a hypocrite because he told others to be honest, whatever the cost, while he himself taught and lived a colossal lie."[181]

Once agnostic C.S. Lewis (1898-1963), wrote in *Mere Christianity*:

> I am trying here to prevent anyone saying the really foolish thing that people often say about Him: "I'm ready to accept Jesus as a great moral teacher, but I don't accept His claim to be God." That is the one thing we must not say. A man who was merely a man and said the sort of things Jesus said would not be a great moral teacher. He would either be a lunatic—on a level with the man who says he is a poached egg—or else he would be the Devil of Hell. You must make your choice. Either this man is, the Son of God: or else a madman or something worse. You can shut Him up for a fool, you can spit at Him and kill Him as a demon; or you can fall at His feet and call Him Lord and God. But let us not come up with any patronizing nonsense about His being a great human teacher. He has not left that open to us. He did not intend to.[182]

If one is to say Jesus is a good moral and ethical teacher, they cannot escape what He taught about Himself. How can He be moral and ethical if He purposely and knowingly lied to others when it came to who He claimed to be, the Son of the Living God?

The testimony of the New Testament, and the testimony of Jesus, is that He was the fulfillment of the Messiah the Old Testament prophets predicted would come. If He claimed to be the promised Messiah, but was not, then how can any of His words be trusted? His moral teachings, and the claim of who He was, cannot be separated from the contention that He is a person of moral excellence.

William G. Moorehead (1836-1914), former president of Xenia Theological Seminary, writes on the necessity of the unity of the two in order for the moral glory of Jesus to be intact. He says, "Christ is the center of all Scripture, as He is the center of all God's purposes and counsels. The four evangelists take up the life and the moral glory of the Son of Man, and they place it alongside of the picture of the Messiah as sketched by the prophets, the historical by the side of the prophetic, and they show how exactly the two match."[183]

The testimony of the New Testament is, that not only was Jesus the prophesied Messiah, He also lived a perfect life. The author of Hebrews writes, "[He] was in all points tempted as we are, yet without sin" (Heb. 4:15).

Jesus Himself, confident of the life He lived, on one occasion challenged His enemies to point out what sin or wrongs he had done! He asked them, "Which of you convicts me of sin? And if I tell the truth, why do you not believe Me?" (John 8:46). Though they wanted to stone Him (John 8:59), His enemies had to turn and walk away because they were unable to bring a charge against Him without lying.

Even the officers who wanted to silence Jesus had to admit, "No man ever spoke like this man" (John 7:46). Those who plotted against Him were even moved by the love He exhibited at the passing of Lazarus. The Bible records their reaction as Jesus wept at the tomb of Lazarus, "See how He loved him!" (John 11:36).

Pilate's wife attested that the Man her husband was about to condemn to death had done nothing wrong, and her husband should have nothing to do with Him. "While [Pilate] was sitting on the judgment seat, his wife sent to him saying, 'Have nothing to do with that just Man, for I have suffered many things today in a dream because of Him'" (Matthew 27:19).

Pilate even confirmed the just character of Jesus. "When Pilate saw that he could not prevail at all, but rather that a tumult was rising, he took water and washed his hands before the multitude, saying, 'I am innocent of the blood of this just Person'" (Matthew 27:25).

One of thieves on the cross affirms that, while he and the other thief deserved death, Jesus had done nothing worthy of suffering crucifixion. The dying thief testified, "And we indeed [die] justly, for we receive the due reward of our deeds; but this Man has done nothing wrong" (Luke 23:41).

As Jesus breathed His last breath one of the soldiers who had helped nail Jesus to the cross, looks up at Him and declares, "Truly, this was the Son of God" (Matthew 27:54).

The testimony of Jesus, and the testimony of others, affirms the moral purity of His life. Concerning the moral perfection of the life of Jesus, Moorehead writes, "His moral glory could not be hid; He could not be less than perfect in everything; it belonged to Him; it was Himself. This moral glory now illumines every page of the four Gospels, as once it did every path He trod."[184]

Because of the moral excellence of His life, one must either accept all that Jesus said and taught, or dismiss it all. He can't be morally pure in one area and be deliberately deceitful in another area without marring His moral excellence in all areas. Philip Schaff (1819-1893), noted historian, writes:

> How, in the name of logic, common sense, and experience, could an imposter—that is deceitful, selfish, depraved mind—have invented, and consistently maintained from the beginning to the end, the purest and noblest character known in history with the most perfect air of truth and reality? How could he have conceived and successfully carried out a plan of unparalleled beneficence, moral magnitude, and sublimity, and sacrifice his own life for it, in the face of the strongest prejudices of his people and age?"[185]

Theologian Alvah Hovey contends that Jesus was an infallible teacher. He writes, "By an 'infallible teacher' is meant one who teaches truth without any mixture of error; or one whose instruction, in whatever form it may be given, will prove, if rightly apprehended, to be wholly correct."[186] He concludes Jesus was such a teacher, further stating, "In view of the facts which we have thus drawn from trustworthy records of Christ's life, we must pronounce Him infallible, and receive all his words as true."[187]

Schaff says, "[Christ's] testimony, if not true, must be downright blasphemy or madness. The former hypothesis cannot stand a moment before the moral purity and dignity of Jesus, revealed in his every word and work, and acknowledged by universal consent."[188] He further adds, "A character so original, so complete, so uniformly consistent, so perfect, so human and yet so high above all human greatness, can be neither a fraud nor a fiction."[189]

One can only conclude that Jesus was a deliberate liar, one who Himself was deceived, or He was the Son of God just as He said and just as the Bible claims. For one cannot separate the moral teachings of Jesus from the claims He made about Himself. Either Jesus was truthful about all He taught, or He was not. Either Jesus was right in all the things He did and said, or He is discredited in all. Who Jesus was, and the message He proclaimed and taught, are inseparable.

Christian historian Kenneth S. Latourette (1884-1968), writes:

> It is not his teachings which make Jesus so remarkable, although these would be enough to give him distinction. It is a combination of the teachings with the man himself. The two cannot be separated . . . It must be obvious to any thoughtful reader of the Gospel records that Jesus regarded himself and his message as inseparable. He was a great teacher, but he was more. His teachings about the kingdom of God, about human conduct, and about God were more important, but they could not be divorced from him without, from his standpoint, being vitiated.[190]

Either the life and teachings of Jesus were/are all true, or they are not. One can't have it both ways, either Jesus is trustworthy in all that He said and did, or it was all a lie, and nothing He said can be trusted to be true. When one honestly examines the evidence, the conclusion can only be that Jesus is Lord. Those who refuse to accept His Lordship do so because, if He is Lord, it has moral implications for their lives. If Christ is Lord, He issues the challenge to live a changed life that answers to a higher authority than self.

To those who will not have a divine Jesus, a divine Savior, will have a Jesus less than what the Bible proclaims about Him and what He Himself claimed to be. To claim a Jesus that is less than what the Bible says about Him and what He says about Himself, is to claim a Jesus who can't be trusted in what He says. He is either Lord or He is not. H.L. Hastings stated in 1890, "Jesus of Nazareth was what he professed to be or he was an imposter."[191]

There may be those in life who suffer from an identity crisis; however, there was absolutely no identity crisis in the life of Jesus Christ. Jesus knew His origin. He knew with certainty who He was. He knew why He came and that His ultimate purpose was the cross. In the totality of His being Jesus never had any doubt He was anyone other than who He said He was—our Lord and Savior

Augustus H. Strong writes, "If Jesus, then, cannot be charged with either mental or moral unsoundness, his testimony must be true, and he himself must be one with God and the revealer of God to men."[192]

In a lecture given on the ethics of Jesus in 1890, John A. Broadus (1827-1895), the eminent Baptist scholar, spoke as only he could:

> [Some] propose to exalt the moral teachings of Jesus by saying that for them no further religion is necessary. They will live by the Sermon on the Mount alone. But he who spoke that great and inspiring discourse gave many other teachings, ethical and spiritual. Were they superfluous? Shall we be really honoring him, or acting wisely and safely for ourselves, if we presume to select one discourse of his and treat all the rest of his teaching and his work as unnecessary and useless?
>
> Besides, who *does* really live up to the Sermon on the Mount? Who can afford to slight the religion of Jesus, upon the assumption of fully conforming to his ethical instructions? To end as we began. He gave ethical and religious teachings together—he stands as not merely a teacher, but a Savior. Others have taught well and helpfully, though not in a way comparable to his teaching, as to

how we ought to live; he alone can also give the spiritual help we need in order actually to live as his teachings require.[193]

Hovey writes, "[The] facts [about Jesus] cannot be reconciled with the hypothesis that he was either a deceiver or self-deceived. They are intelligible and credible only on the supposition that he was what he claimed to be, a humble, holy, infallible Being."[194]

Strong echoes the words of Hovey, "The absolute purity of his conscience, the humility of his spirit, the self-denying beneficence of his life, show this hypothesis [that he was a deceiver or self-deceived] to be incredible." [195]

For one to see Jesus as only a great moral teacher and nothing else is to miss the greater reason of His mission. Harvie Branscomb says, "Jesus will never mean anything to anyone who is not willing to take Him as He actually was . . . There are a number of indications that Jesus did not regard Himself primarily as a teacher and that His work of teaching was entirely subordinate to a larger objective, [the redemption of humanity]."[196]

The moral life and teachings of Jesus being attested to as being superior, even by those who may not yield their spiritual allegiance to Him, is a remarkable admission to His uniqueness. Yet, Strong succinctly writes, "[Jesus] sought to be Lord, rather than Teacher only."[197]

The very fact that non-believers acknowledge and hail Jesus as a moral and ethical teacher is an affirmation that the life He lived, and the words He spoke, are true, not just in part, but in whole. If not, He could not be an example of moral excellence or man's Savior and Lord.

Morehead writes, "That the moral glory of Jesus Christ as set forth in the four Gospels cannot be the product of the unaided human intellect, that only the Spirit of God is competent to execute this matchless portrait of the Son of Man."[198]

Such an affirmation regarding the moral life of Jesus and His teachings is a compelling truth that the Bible is divinely inspired. As shall be seen in the next chapter, to those who embrace such an affirmation, a changed life will result.

CHAPTER 11
CHANGED LIVES AFFIRM BIBLE'S INSPIRATION

In the early 1980's, this writer was pastor of a rural church in eastern North Carolina. Living in the community, where the church was located, were two brothers who participated on a regular basis in activities that were self-destructive to themselves and their families. Neither had any interest in Christianity, the church, or the Bible. One of the brothers, at the urging of family and friends, begin going to church. He listened to the message being proclaimed that Christ came to earth to die for humanities sins, that He came to remove man's guilt, forgive his sins, give him inward peace, and change his life.

As this young man listened to this radical message it struck a chord in a heart that had grown weary of living a lifestyle that left him empty on the inside. In time he responded to the invitation of Christ, "Come unto Me, all you who labor and are heavy laden, and I will give you rest." (Matthew 11:28). Tired of his sin, and under the wooing of the Holy Spirit, he came before the Lord with a contrite heart and asked the Lord, who inhabits eternity, to come dwell in his life. His life was radically changed from that day forward.

His life was so radically changed that those who knew him were amazed at what had happened. One of those who were amazed was his own brother. No longer were they participating together in the same self-destructive style. His brother, not fully grasping what had happened to his older brother finally remarked to him, "I have never really believed all this stuff about Jesus and the Bible. I have always found ways to explain it all away, but there is one thing I can't explain away is your changed life. One thing is certain, you are not the person you used to be; your life has dramatically changed."

The eighth compelling argument for the truthfulness of the Bible being the divinely inspired Word of God is the changed lives that have resulted from those who believe and embrace its message.

Ever since Jesus Christ stepped from eternity into time in the form of a man, He has been about the business of changing lives. Paul stated, "If any man is in Christ, he is a new creation, old things have passed away; behold, all things have become new" (2 Cor. 5:17). What happened to the young man who bowed his knee to Jesus Christ is what happens to all, whom with a sincere heart, bow before the King of kings; they become new creations in Him. The younger brother, in acknowledging his brother had changed, verified the fulfillment of 2 Corinthians 5:17.

When a person's heart is awakened by the Holy Spirit to its need of forgiveness of sin, and responds to the proclamation of the biblical message of God's redemptive work accomplished in Jesus Christ, a changed life will occur. Jeremiah and Ezekiel both prophesied this life changing transformation would be made possible when the Messiah would come. Ezekiel wrote, "Thus says the Lord God . . . then I will give them one heart, and I will put a new spirit within them, and I will take the stony heart out of their flesh, and will give than an heart of flesh" (Ez. 11:19). Jeremiah wrote that the day would come when the Lord would put His law "in their inward parts, and write it in their hearts" (Jer. 31:33).

The Messiah's coming would make it possible for man's heart to be changed. The heart, that part of man on the inside where decisions are made, where he says "yes" and "no," where his will is, where his likes and dislikes are formed. This possibility of transforming the heart, as prophesied by Jeremiah and Ezekiel, finds fulfillment in Jesus Christ.

Since Christ's birth, life, death on the cross, His resurrection, and ascension back to heaven, countless millions have responded to the message that He can transform lives, and have had their lives changed. Every life changed, as a result of responding to the biblical message of Christ, gives witness to His redemptive mission, and also affirms the divine inspiration of the Bible which proclaims that redemptive mission.

Libraries could not hold all the pages of those who have had their lives transformed by the life changing message of the Bible. In this chapter a few examples will be given of the lives that have been radically changed by the message of Christ, affirming the veracity of the Bible as being divinely inspired.

Many examples of lives that were transformed while Christ walked on earth could be cited, but the focus here will be narrowed to lives that were changed after the resurrection of Christ. The few examples that follow are only representative voices, each speaking on behalf of the millions who have also experienced the transformation found in the redemptive message of Christ.

The Disciples

As Christ's lifeless body lay in the cold, damp tomb following His crucifixion, the disciples were hiding behind locked doors. Three days after the death of Christ, these fearful disciples became men no longer fearful of governmental authorities, but boldly proclaiming the message, "Christ lives!" What brought about such a remarkable change in these men's lives?

French skeptic, Ernest Renan, explained the amazing change that took place in the disciples this way, "Jesus died, and there was no objective appearance even of his spirit. Mary Magdalene was the victim of subjective hallucination, and her hallucination became contagious."[199] What great lengths skeptics will go to attempt to explain away the resurrection of Christ!

A hallucination could not fuel their new found passion and enthusiasm. A hallucination would eventually fade in its vision. However, something happened that resulted in the vision they had of Christ not fading. What happened was the resurrected Christ personally appeared to them (Luke 24:36-53; John 20:19-31). Remaining on earth forty days after his resurrection, and before His ascension, the disciples received much instruction from Jesus during that time (Acts 1:1-11).

It was visibly seeing the resurrected Christ that transformed the disciples, from being fearful, to being fearless men who "turned the world upside down" (Acts 17:6). Instead of the disciples being afraid of governmental authority, the government authorities became afraid of them (Acts 4:13-22). When the facts are examined, foolish explanations such as Renan's for the disciples transformation, give way to what really transpired; the resurrected Christ "opened He their understanding, that they might understand the scriptures" (Luke 24;45).

Apostle Paul

One of the most dramatic transformations of a life found in the Bible, as well as the most unlikely, is that of Saul of Tarsus whose name was changed to Paul (Acts 9:11). Paul was born in Tarsus and was a Jew's Jew, being steeped in the Jewish orthodoxy. By profession he as a tentmaker (Acts 18:3), but he was passionate about his Jewish faith. He writes that he was "circumcised the eighth day, of the stock of Israel, of the tribe of Benjamin, a Hebrew of the Hebrews; as touching the law a Pharisee; concerning zeal, persecuting the church; concerning the righteousness which is in the law, blameless" (Philippians 3:5-6).

We first meet the man Saul in Acts 8, where he was consenting to the death of Stephen (Acts 8:1). He believed Christianity was a threat to Judaism, and did what he could to persecuting Christians within the early church. He was "breathing out threatenings and slaughter against the disciples of the Lord" (Acts 9:1). One day Saul, who became Paul, was on his way to Damascus "that if he found any who were of the Way [Christians], whether they were men or women, he might bring them bound to Jerusalem" (Acts 9:2).

As he got close to Damascus, the resurrected Christ appeared unto Paul. Kneeling before the living Jesus, on a hot and dusty road, he surrendered to the King of Kings and Lord of Lords (Acts 9). From that day forward Paul was a changed man. Instead of persecuting those who followed Christ, he was now proclaiming Christ as the only way of salvation. Called to carry the message of Christ to the Gentiles, he carried it not only to them, but to Jew and Gentile alike. As one follows Paul on his missionary journeys in Acts, he was the first missionary in Europe (Acts 16:6-9), and preached in most of the known world of the day, organizing churches wherever he went. Only eternity will reveal the lives that were changed as the result of Paul's life being drastically changed.

From a man who persecuted Christians, to a man who boldly proclaimed Christ, he wrote thirteen books of the twenty-seven in the New Testament. Interestingly, when change first occurred in Paul's life, it was so unexpected, those who were Christians thought it was only deception on his part so he could infiltrate the church to persecute more Christians (Acts 9:13-14; 26-27). How does one explain such a dramatic change taking place in Paul's life? Paul answers the question himself with the verse with which we began this chapter, "If any man be in Christ, old things are passed away, behold; all things become new" (2 Corinthians 5:17). Paul's radical transformation affirms both the sufficiency of Christ to change a life, and the sufficiency of the biblical message to place a call on one's life to embrace Christ.

Augustine

In the fourth century, the Word of God pierced and transformed the heart of a man named Augustine (354-430). Born in Northern Africa, his father was a pagan and his mother was a Christian. His mother sought to influence him, but he became involved in a life of immorality, taking a mistress, and even fathered a child.

Known for his rhetoric, he became a teacher of renown, teaching in Thagaste, Carthage, Rome, and Milan. At age thirty, he for a time, adopted skepticism, but he could never escape the lack of peace in his soul. In 386, he came to a spiritual crossroads in his life. In *The Confessions Of Saint Augustine,* he tells of the encounter that transformed his life:

> I cast myself down I know not how, under a certain fig-tree, giving full vent to my tears; and the floods of mine eyes gushed out an acceptable sacrifice to Thee. And, not indeed in these words, yet to this purpose, spoke I much unto Thee: and Thou, O Lord, how long? how long, Lord, wilt Thou be angry forever? Remember not our former iniquities, for I felt that I was held by them. I sent up these sorrowful words: How long, how long, "to-morrow, and

tomorrow?" Why not now? why not is there this hour an end to my uncleanness? So was I speaking and weeping in the most bitter contrition of my heart, when, lo! I heard from a neighboring house a voice, as of boy or girl, I know not, chanting, and oft repeating, "Take up and read; Take up and read." Instantly, my countenance altered, I began to think most intently whether children were wont in any kind of play to sing such words: nor could I remember ever to have heard the like. So checking the torrent of my tears, I arose; interpreting it to be no other than a command from God to open the book, and read the first chapter I should find. For I had heard of Antony, that coming in during the reading of the Gospel, he received the admonition, as if what was being read was spoken to him: Go, sell all that thou hast, and give to the poor, and thou shalt have treasure in heaven, and come and follow me: and by such oracle he was forthwith converted unto Thee. Eagerly then I returned to the place where Alypius was sitting; for there had I laid the volume of the Apostle when I arose thence. I seized, opened, and in silence read that section on which my eyes first fell: Not in rioting and drunkenness, not in chambering and wantonness, not in strife and envying; but put ye on the Lord Jesus Christ, and make not provision for the flesh, in concupiscence (Romans 13:13-14). No further would I read; nor needed I: for instantly at the end of this sentence, by a light as it were of serenity infused into my heart, all the darkness of doubt vanished away.[200]

From that day forward his life was never the same. He moved back to North Africa in 388, and entering the priesthood, he later became the Bishop of Hippo. He devoted the rest of his life in the living and defense of the Christian faith, becoming one of the most influential thinkers the Church has ever produced. A man once given to immorality and skepticism, many of his theological and philosophical writings are unsurpassed even to this day. His five proofs for the existence of God are still the standard in apologetics for a logical and reasoned argument for God's existence.

Time and space forbids listing all the accomplishments and the scope of the influence Augustine had, and is still having. What brought about this transformation in his life? It was the whispering Voice from the divinely inspired Word of God, and, using Augustine's own words, "infused" peace and life within his soul.

Martin Luther

In Germany, a man named Martin Luther (1483-1546), was searching for inward peace but could not find it. In 1505, in his search for inner peace, and after being struck by lightning, Luther became a monk in hopes of finding elusive peace in his soul. However, the torment in his soul would not go away. Following the rituals and practices of the Roman Church did not relieve his tormented soul, but actually created more inner despair.

Longing to obtain the righteousness of God, he began reading the Bible in hopes of finding relief. Finally, one day while reading in Romans, Luther found the inner peace for which he sought. He recounts of the joyous day:

> The words "righteous" and "righteousness of God" struck my conscience like lightning. When I heard them I was exceedingly terrified. If God is righteous, I thought, He must punish. But when by God's grace I pondered . . . over the words, "He who through faith is righteous shall live" (Romans 1:17) and "the righteousness of God" (Romans 3:21), I soon came to the conclusion that if we, as righteous men, ought to live from faith and if the righteousness of God should contribute to the salvation of all who believe, then salvation will not be our merit but God's mercy. My spirit was thereby cheered. For it is by the righteousness of God that we are justified and saved through Christ. These words which had before terrified me now became more pleasing to me. The Holy Spirit unveiled the Scripture for me . . . When I discovered the proper distinction—namely,

that the law is one thing and the gospel is another—I made myself free.[201]

From that day forward Luther's life was transformed. The Word of God, as it made its way from the printed page to his heart, changed his life. He realized, if the biblical message was right, then the Roman Catholic Church's teaching that salvation was bestowed by the merits of man was wrong. Luther sought to reform the church, but his efforts were met with resistance. Eventually, he was excommunicated by the pope in January 1521.

At the Diet of Worms on April 18, 1521, Luther was asked to recant his views that criticized the Roman Church. Luther responded, "I am bound by the Scriptures I have quoted and my conscience is captive to the Word of God. I cannot and will not retract anything, since it is neither safe nor right to go against conscience . . . Here I stand; I cannot do otherwise."[202]

Through Luther's efforts, the Protestant Reformation was born, which changed the course of Christianity throughout the world. No longer was the Roman hierarchy seen as authoritative, but it was now Sola Scriptura. Luther's whole intent was to "reform" the Church anew according to the Word of God, for Scripture to be the guide.

As the result of a monk being transformed by the message of Scripture, the course of Christianity was transformed as well. What happened to Luther, and what was accomplished through him, was more than the work of man, but the result of the transforming power of the divinely inspired Bible effecting human history.

Charles Spurgeon

Born in England in 1834, was Charles Spurgeon, who like Luther, could not find peace in his soul. Growing-up in a Christian home, his grandfather and father were preachers. Even with the privilege of having such an influence upon his life, it did not ease his agony of heart. One snowy day in January of 1850, the peace he longed for was found and his life radically changed. Spurgeon tells in his own words what happened.

At last, one snowy day, it snowed so much I could not go the place I had determined to go to, and I was obliged to stop on the road, and it was a blessed stop to me, I found rather an obscure street, and turned down a court, and there was a little chapel. I wanted to go somewhere, but I did not know this place. It was the Primitive Methodist Chapel . . . I wanted to know how I might be saved . . . So, sitting down, the service went on but no minster came; at last a very thin-looking man came into the pulpit and opened his Bible, and read these words: "Look unto me and be ye saved, all the ends of the earth" [Isaiah 45:22]. Just setting his eyes upon me, as if he knew all my heart, he said, "Young man, you are in trouble." Well, I was sure enough. Says he, "You will never get out of it unless you look to Christ." And then, lifting up his hands, he cried out as only a Primitive Methodist could do, "Look, look, look! It is only look," said he. I saw at once the way of salvation. Oh, how I did leap for joy at that moment . . . I had been waiting to do fifty things, but when I heard this word, "Look," what a charming word it seemed to me! Oh, I looked until I could almost have looked my eyes away; and in heaven I will look on still in my joy unutterable![203]

With his life changing look toward Christ, he was not only transformed, but during his life he transformed the spiritual landscape of England. Eventually becoming pastor of the great Metropolitan Tabernacle, he preached to thousands upon thousands over the course of his life. His writings were numerous, and his sermons made their way into print and were circulated far and wide, reaching thousands more. His golden tongue, and the eloquence of his words, found him being called the "Prince of Preachers."[204] When he died in 1892, he left behind a multitude of writings and sermons that are still being printed and read today.

A simple message, on a snowy day, from Isaiah 45:22, was heard by a young Spurgeon and it transformed his life. The mere words of a man could not have done so, but words spoken from a Book divinely inspired could.

George Mueller

Born in Germany, like Martin Luther, was George Mueller (1805–1898).[205] Mueller's father wanted him to be a clergyman, but the lifestyle he adopted was one of debauchery and bad habits. Muller says his teenage years were, "days of sin." One night, while attending a Bible study in the home of a friend, Muller's life was touched by what he saw and heard, and at age twenty his life was transformed. Beginning a lifetime of meditation on the Scriptures, he sensed a call to be a missionary. Moving to England, he became involved in various missionary endeavors.

His belief in the sufficiency of the Bible for faith and practice, he founded the Scriptural Knowledge Institution for Home and Abroad, endeavoring to spread an understanding of the Scriptures. In 1836, he began an orphanage which he headed-up until his death in 1898. The foundation of the orphanage was based on Philippians 4:19, "And my God shall supply all your needs according to His riches in glory by Christ Jesus."

Mueller and his wife prayed over every need that arose in the orphanage. Never, in over sixty years, did they see any need, whether it was supplies, food, or money, go unmet. He came to be known as "the man who gets things from God."[206] He kept a diary of the many answers to prayers he experienced during his life, saying he knew of some 50,000 direct answers!

A man who stated he read the Bible through over 200 times, he based his whole ministry on the sufficiency of the promises of God as found in the Bible to meet the needs of the orphanage. The transformation that occurred in George Mueller's life, and throughout his ministry, was an affirmation that the Bible is the divinely inspired Word of God.

John Colby

One of the most fascinating stories about the life changing power of Jesus Christ, told by Augustus H. Strong (1836-1921), is the conversion of John Colby. Colby was the brother-in-law of Daniel Webster (1782-1852). The story was related to Strong by Peter Harvey, who was a friend of Webster. Webster, an early American statesman, and Harvey visited John Colby, and Harvey later penned what they both witnessed on their visit. While this is lengthy, it is worth repeating as it gives testimony of the transforming power of the Christ of the Bible. Strong writes:

> Mr. Peter Harvey was a lifelong friend of Daniel Webster. He tells how one John Colby married the oldest sister of Mr. Webster. Mr. Webster said of John Colby: "Finally he went to Andover, New Hampshire, and there bought a farm. The only recollection I have about him is that he was called the wickedest man in the neighborhood, so far as swearing and impiety went. I used to wonder how my sister could marry so profane a man as John Colby." Years afterwards news comes to Mr. Webster that a wonderful change has passed upon John Colby. Mr. Harvey and Mr. Webster take a journey together to visit John Colby. As Mr. Webster enters John Colby's house, he sees open before him a large-print Bible, which he has just been reading. When greetings have been interchanged, the first question John Colby asks of Mr. Webster is, "Are you a Christian?" And then, at John Colby's suggestion, the two men kneel and pray together. When the visit is done, this is what Mr. Webster says to Mr. Harvey as they ride away: "I should like to know what the enemies of religion would say to John Colby's conversion? There was a man as unlikely, humanly speaking, to become a Christian as any man I ever saw. He was reckless, heedless, and impious, never attended church, never experienced the good influence of associating with religious people. And here he has been living on in that reckless way until he has got to be an old man, until a period of life when you naturally would not expect his habits to change. And yet he has been brought into the condition in which we have seen him today, a penitent, trusting, humble believer." "Whatever people may say," added Mr. Webster, "nothing can convince me that anything short of the grace of Almighty God could make such a change as I, with my own eyes, have witnessed in the life of John Colby." When they got back to Franklin,

New Hampshire, in the evening, they met another lifelong friend of Mr. Webster's, John Taylor, standing at his door. Mr. Webster called out: "Well, John Taylor miracles happen in these latter days as well as in the days of old." "What now, Squire?" asked John Taylor. "Why," replied Mr. Webster, "John Colby has become a Christian. If that is not a miracle, what is?"[207]

Another life miraculously transformed by the power to the Gospel message. No amount of human verbiage can explain away such a remarkable change in John Colby's life, other than the power of the living Word through the written Word making way into his heart.

R.A. Torrey

Ruben Archer (R.A.) Torrey (1856-1928), who was a skeptic in his early years, eventually became a defender of the faith.[208] Born in New Jersey, and reared in a Christian home, he desired to pursue the path of being a lawyer. Entering Yale University, he became a skeptic and became involved in cards, dancing, race tracks, the theater, and other worldly pursuits. Such a life drove him to despair and on the verge of suicide. One night he sought to take his life, but his mother was praying for him at that very moment, and, as result, his urge to take his life turned into an urge to pray. That night as a nineteen year old, in 1875, he surrendered to the Lord to do whatever He would have him do.

He abandoned his studies to be a lawyer, and entered Yale Divinity School to study for the ministry. The once skeptic now had a burning desire to tell others about Christ. A man who was proficient in both Greek and Hebrew, he become a defender of the faith against liberalism. A skilled orator, he teamed with D.L. Moody in the latter part of his ministry. He was much in demand as a speaker, and traveled the world proclaiming the unsearchable riches of Christ. For a time, he was pastor of the Moody Memorial Church, the first overseer of what came to be known as Moody Bible Institute, and dean of the Los Angeles Bible Institute.

The accomplishments of this gifted man are endless. How would one explain how a man who used to be a skeptic and who pursued worldly pleasures, become a man who preached on numerous occasions the sermon entitled, *Ten Reasons Why I Believe the Bible is the Word of God*. His skepticism was burned away by the eternal fire of the divinely inspired Bible, whose flame forever burns brightly.

Mel Trotter

When one speaks of the Bible's message having the ability to change a life, few can be more remarkable than the transformation of Mel Trotter (1870-1940).[209] There have been few men who have lived so hopeless a life as Trotter. So given over to alcohol, there were times he was so drunk he didn't know his name. He began drinking heavily by age nineteen, and it only got worse.

One winter night in January of 1897, Trotter staggered into a rescue mission in Chicago. Listening in a drunken stupor to a man give his testimony about how Christ can change lives, that night he asked Christ to change his life. He was never the same again, living the rest of his life by 2 Corinthians 5:17. For two years, after his amazing transformation, he dedicated himself to memorizing as much as the Bible as possible. This former drunkard became known as "the man who raved about Jesus."[210]

Becoming an ordained minister in 1905, he was much in demand for telling his testimony of the transforming of Christ. In addition to his evangelistic ministry, Trotter helped organize numerous rescue missions for the purpose of helping men and women just like himself. "The man who raved about Jesus," did so until his death in 1940.

Try as the skeptic may, there is no natural explanation for the amazing transformation of Mel Trotter. His change was one that was not the result of man simply turning over a new leaf, but it was the result of him having an encounter with the Living Word of God as proclaimed in the divinely inspired written Word of God.

Billy Graham

On November 7, 1918, in Charlotte, North Carolina, born into the home of parents who were dairy farmers, was a baby boy who would one day dine with kings, queens, and presidents, and speak around the world.[211] Such humble beginnings gave no indication of what lay ahead for the boy whose parents named him Billy. Growing up on a dairy farm, Billy Graham knew the meaning of hard work. While his parents took him to church, he was involved more in helping on the farm and school activities than a commitment to Christ.

In 1934, a preacher by the name of Mordecai Ham came to Charlotte to hold a series of evangelistic meetings that lasted eleven weeks. Rev. Ham had made a decision under the ministry of the famous D.L. Moody. Billy and his parents went to hear this dynamic preacher. As Rev. Ham proclaimed the life changing message from the Bible night after night, the Living Word made its way into the heart of sixteen year old Billy Graham. Resisting for a while, the Voice that was speaking to him about his need of Christ, he finally answered the invitation to come to Christ when Rev. Ham quoted from Romans, "But God commended His love toward us, in that, while we were sinners Christ died for us" (Rom. 5:8).

Soon after coming to Christ, Graham sensed the call of God on his life to enter the ministry. Attending Bob Jones College, Florida Bible Institute, and later Wheaton College in Illinois, after graduation in 1943, he pastored for awhile, and even served as president of Northwestern College for four years. A Southern Baptist, his booming, clear voice made him a revival favorite.

He began conducting evangelistic crusades in 1948, and in 1950 formed the Billy Graham Evangelistic Association, becoming a full-time conservative Christian evangelist. Graham has held crusades all over the world, with literally millions hearing the transforming message of Christ he proclaimed from the Bible. For more than seventy years Billy Graham has been a name known and respected around the world. A man who has dined with kings and queens, he is comfortable with a pauper or a prince. He has met and prayed with every President since Harry S. Truman.

How could one explain the astounding worldwide influence that has resulted from a life of such humble beginnings? It all began when the Voice, from the life giving Word of God, found its way into his heart and transformed his life at age sixteen. At that moment, a divine Hand guided his life in paths that otherwise would never have been possible. Billy Graham's journey in life, and in ministry, affirms once again, as it has over and over again in innumerable lives, that the Bible is the divinely inspired Word of God.

Daniel Merritt

In 1970, an unlikely transformation took place in the life of an eighteen year old college freshman. The young man was an introvert, whose life was consumed with sports and striving to become better at his chosen sport of distance running. One night, though, he found himself attending an evangelistic crusade and listening to the speaker preach a message on being, "religious but lost." Growing-up attending church, this young man had his heart pricked as he realized he had religion, but not a personal relationship with Jesus Christ. During the hymn of invitation he made his way down front, and that night bowed his knee to Jesus Christ, received His forgiveness and a changed heart.

This introverted young man soon sensed a call to preach the gospel. Of all people, surely not this shy young man. However, the power of Christ can radically change someone. Yielding to the call to preach the unsearchable riches of Christ, this once introverted young man became an extrovert by the changing power of Christ, and has now been preaching the life changing message of Christ for over forty years. This writer knows personally the person who experienced this life changing transformation, for it is his own personal story.

For four decades, this writer has seen the ability of the power of the Word of God to transform lives. There have been witnessed the immoral made pure, the drunk made sober, the drug addict made clean, the thief made honest, the hateful made loving, the liar made truthful, and the religious brought into a living relationship with Jesus Christ. This writer has had affirmed, in his own mind, that the Bible is the divinely inspired Word of God.

Yes, the message of Christ, as found in the Bible, can transform lives. There could be a continuation of looking at the lives that have been transformed by the proclamation of the written Word, giving testimony of the Living Word. There is not enough printers ink to write about all the lives that have been changed by the message of the Bible.

As the life giving Words from the pages of the Bible are transferred into the heart of an individual by the Holy Spirit, a transformation takes place that can't be explained or achieved by human wisdom. Atheism cannot transform a life, it only makes a fool out of the individual (Ps. 14:1). Islam cannot transform a life, it only enslaves the soul. Buddhism cannot transform a life, it only burdens the spirit. Hinduism cannot transform a life, it only removes the dignity of man. Communism cannot transform a life, it only oppresses those it embraces. Deciding to turn over a new leaf will not transform a life, it will only leads to frustration. The best human philosophies of man cannot transform a life, they only confuse the mind. Only the Word of God can take a sinner and make them a new creation.

Countless millions, whose lives have been transformed by the proclamation of the One the Bible calls man's Redeemer, is a compelling argument for the truthfulness of the Bible as being divinely inspired.

CHAPTER 12
CONCLUSION
FAITH VERSUS REASON

It has been the purpose of this book to examine eight compelling truths which affirm the truthfulness of the Bible as being the divinely inspired Word of God. After laying a foundation in regard to representative voices from the camps of skeptics, liberal theologians, and conservative theologians as to their views regarding biblical inspiration; there was an examining as to the Bible's claim of being inspired; and then there were witnesses from within and outside of the Bible who affirmed its inspiration.

Having laid a foundation, there were then examined eight reasonable, compelling arguments that attest to the Bible being the divinely inspired Word: thematic unity, mathematical unity, fulfilled prophecy, archaeological evidence, its indestructibility, its practicality for living, the moral life and teachings of Jesus, and changed lives.

It is recognized, not every question was answered or every area exhaustively examined. Such a task would go beyond the scope and the purpose of this work. It has been the purpose here to affirm that there are some reasonable arguments the honest inquirer cannot easily explain away, nor dismiss as merely being coincidence or the product of man's wisdom.

One would have to be close minded not to recognize that there is a Higher Mind behind the writing of the Bible; it is not simply the genius of the authors. To one who is open to knowing the truth, upon careful contemplation, the obvious is hard to reject in the face of the

177

abundance of evidence that exists regarding whether or not the Bible is divinely inspired. John W. Montgomery writes, "If you reject Him it will not be because of a deficiency of evidence but because of a perversity of will."[212]

While in college, this writer learned from obtaining a minor in philosophy, truth can be known if three conditions combine and merge as one. They are: (1) the actual existence of that which is claimed to be true; (2) the capacity and ability of man's mind to know and grasp truth; and (3) and the provision of some way or means by which that truth can be communicated to the mind.[213]

One can know the truth of God's existence and His unfolding purpose as He has revealed it in the Bible, because He actually does exist; man was created by the Creator with a mind able to grasp and know truth; and through compelling arguments or evidences that cannot be explained away by human reason alone and the illumination of the Holy Spirit, truth can be communicated to the mind.

The question is not whether or not there are logical, compelling arguments that affirm the Bible's inspiration, the question is whether man is willing to submit himself to the Creator who has taken the initiative to reveal Himself in the Bible. The problem is not whether truth can be known or not, but it is a matter that man chooses to live independently of God. Man desires to live autonomously.

Ultimately, the problem of man is that he does not want to yield his prideful autonomy to the authority of the One who created him, and who has revealed in His Word what is the best path for him to follow in order for him to realize true fulfillment which all seek. Man's own sinful heart is a barrier that can keep God hidden, and can result in him rejecting what presents itself to be convincing and compelling arguments or proofs for the truthfulness of the Bible as being divinely inspired.

It is understood, ultimately one must yield in faith to that which has been revealed, and therein lays another problem for man. Man perceives there is a conflict between faith and reason, yet true faith is founded upon reason. Faith is more than a "leap in the dark," as Kierkegaard contended, but faith is based upon reasonable facts. Faith and reason are two pillars of the Christian belief system. Christianity is anchored in reasonable, reasoned conclusions that lead one after examining the evidence to conclude, "This is true."

Faith is not throwing one's mind in neutral; faith is founded upon reasonable facts and proofs. Blaise Pascal (1623-1662), writes that reason is not to be tossed aside, "On the contrary, the mind must be open to proofs, must be confirmed by custom, and offer itself in humbleness to inspiration . . ."[214]

Skeptics speak of the unreasonableness of faith, that it is not anchored in reasonableness. However, it is the "faith" of the skeptic that is not anchored in reasonableness. Even in the face of reasonable evidence or proofs, the skeptic puts his faith in that which he wishes and hopes not to be true.

This writer has always been intrigued by the fact skeptics and atheists are continually attempting to prove something that doesn't exist, while dismissing sound reasonable arguments that clearly affirm the existence of an Intelligent Designer. Why the obsession of seeking to prove something that doesn't exist? The whole heart of the matter was best stated by Pascal when he said, "[T]he mind must be open to proofs."

In regard to those who assert and embrace skepticism, Norman Geisler writes:

> The overall skeptical attempt to suspend all judgment about reality is self-defeating; since it implies a judgment about reality . . . Complete skepticism is self-defeating. The very affirmation that all truth is unknowable is itself presented as a truth affirmation. As a truth statement purporting that no truth statements can be made, it undercuts itself.[215]

When one begins from a presupposition that is not honestly searching for the truth, but has pre-decided not to believe, no amount of proofs will suffice. If man is looking for reasons not to believe, and for reasons to reject the truth, the inclination of man's autonomous nature will hide the Light from his eyes. Paul K. Jewett has written, "The denial of the truths of faith is, in the last analysis, no less a faith than faith itself, for it rests on personal assumptions which are apart from scientific necessity."[216]

For one who honestly inquires to know what has already been revealed, their search will result in reasoned faith. Jewett further states, "As the truth of reason carries its own evidences, so also with faith . . . The only sufficient ground of faith is the authority of God himself as He addresses me in His Word."[217]

Genuine Christianity is one of rational faith. J.I. Packer writes, "Whereas the non-Christian is led by faithless reason, the Christian should be guided by reasoning faith."[218] The Christian faith does not hinder the freedom of one's reasoning powers. The opposite is true, the Christian faith enables one to be free to properly reason. Expanding upon and explaining this truth, Packer writes:

> Tossed about by every cross-currents of reaction, man without God is not free for truth; he is forever mastered by the things he takes for granted, the victim of a hopeless and everlasting relativism. Only as his thoughts are searched, challenged and correct by God through His Word may man hope to rise to a way of looking at things which, instead of reflecting merely passing phases of human thought, reflects God's eternal truth. This is the only road to intellectual freedom, and its sole safeguard is the principle of absolute subjection to Scripture.[219]

Truth is not created, it is discovered. The Christian faith is founded on what the Bible affirms to be true. The truths found in the Bible are known because God took the initiative to reveal Himself to man, making it possible for him to discover those truths. The revelation of truths contained in the Bible is sufficient for man to discover and know the Living God. Alvah Hovey writes:

> Even God approaches men as those who can and must judge for themselves. He never demands faith without sufficient evidence . . . Human reason may have convincing evidence that something infinite exists, though it has never

comprehended the infinite; just as it may have convincing evidence that many things exist which, though not strictly infinite, are known to transcend human knowledge.[220]

It is true, there will always be an element of tension between faith and reason, or as Kierkegaard says, "a paradoxicalness," yet the two are Siamese twins. One can't adequately exist without the other. Faith is an act of the will, but it is also an act of the intellect.

Theologian Augustus H. Strong contends reason and faith cannot be separated. He writes,

> Faith is knowledge, and a higher sort of knowledge. Faith discovers facts and relations, but it does not create them . . . Faith is the trustworthiness of our faculties to that which has been revealed to us. Knowledge and faith cannot be severed from one another. Faith is not antithetical to knowledge; it is rather a larger and more fundamental sort of knowledge . . . Faith then is the highest knowledge, because it is the act of the integral soul, the insight, not of one eye alone, but two eyes of the mind, intellect and love to God.[221]

Upon examining the claims of the Bible, and the reasonableness of the arguments presented, man is faced with a decision. As the Lord reveals Himself in the pages of the Bible, He issues to humanity the invitation He issued to Matthew, "Follow me" (Luke 5:27). Man can either, like Adam, hide from the Lord, or like Matthew, rise up and follow Him.

Man has not been left to himself to stumble in the dark in an attempt to discover who God is; God has revealed Himself in the Written Word and the Living Word, Jesus Christ. It is in the Bible, God's Word, that one finds within its pages a God who has revealed His redemptive plan in Jesus Christ and how one should live once that redemptive plan has been embraced in one's life.

Geisler succinctly writes concerning the revelation of God as found in the Bible:

With these sixty-six books we have the complete and final revelation of God for the faith and practice of believers . . . The point is that the Bible and the Bible alone contains all doctrinal and ethical truth God has revealed to mankind. And the Bible alone is the canon or norm for all truth. All other alleged truth must be brought to the bar of Holy Scripture to be tested. The Bible and the Bible alone, all sixty-six books, has been confirmed by God through Christ to be His infallible Word.[222]

Is the Bible fiction, fables, or fact? The Apostle Peter answers, "For we did not follow cunningly devised fables when we made known to you the power and coming of our Lord Jesus Christ, but were eyewitnesses of His majesty" (2 Peter 1:16).

To the honest and inquiring mind that is seeking to know the truth, not one who is seeking to suppress the truth or deny it, there are reasonable and compelling arguments that affirm the Bible is the divinely inspired Word of God. God has communicated to man; it is now the responsibility of man to respond to His revealed communication.

Strong writes, "Water is of little use to man if he will not drink . . . Though we cannot earn salvation, we must take it; and in this taking it involves a surrender of heart and life which ensure union with Christ."[223]

Isaiah issues an open invitation to humanity, "Ho! Everyone who thirsts, Come to the waters; and you who have no money, Come, buy and eat; yes, Come, buy wine and milk without money and without price" (Isaiah 55:1).

Christ has paid the price for man's sin; He has provided the water that will quench the thirst of man's soul. All one must do is come and drink. The invitation has been issued.

To those who sense their need of Christ, who has come to believe He is able and willing to forgive and transform them, who cast themselves unreservedly upon His mercy and grace, and trust Him alone for salvation, He will receive with open arms.

Come, He is waiting.

What will the response be?

Bibliography

BOOKS:

Augustine. *The Confessions of Saint Augustine*. Trans. R.S. Pine-Coffin. New York: Penguin Group, 1961.

Beeson, Ray and Ranelda M. Hunsicker. *The Hidden Price of Greatness*. Wheaton, Illinois: Tyndale House Publishers, 1991.

Branscomb, Harvie. *The Teachings of Jesus*. New York: Abingdon Press, 1959.

Brooks Keith L. *Overwhelming Mathematical Evidence of the Divine Inspiration of the Scriptures*. Syracuse, New York: Book Fellowship, n.d.

Carroll, B.H. *Inspiration of the Bible*. New York: Revell, 1930.

Choron, Jacques. *The Romance of Philosophy*. New York, New York: The MacMillan Company, 1963.

Conwell, Russell H. *The Life of Charles Haddon Spurgeon*. Edgewood Publishing Company, 1892.

Craigie, Peter C. *The Problem of War in the Old Testament*. Grand Rapids, Michigan: William B. Eerdmans Company, 1978.

Criswell, W.A. *Expository Sermons on Revelation*. Grand Rapids, Michigan: Zondervan Publishing Company, 1962.

Culpepper, Robert H. *Interpreting the Atonement*. Grand Rapids, Michigan: William B. Eerdmans Publishing Company, 1966.

DeMoss, Nancy L., ed. *The Rebirth of America*. Philadelphia, PA: Arthur S. DeMoss Foundation, 1986.

Dillenberger, John, and Claude Welch. *Protestant Christianity*. New York, New York: Charles Scribner's Sons, 1954.

Dockery, David S. *The Doctrine of the Bible*. Nashville, Tennessee: Seminary Extension, 1997.

Dollar, Turman, Jerry Falwell, A.V. Henderson, and Jack Hyles. Eds. *Building Blocks of the Faith*. Nashville, Tennessee: Fundamentalist Church Publications, 1977.

Dowey, Edward. A. Dowey, Jr.*The Knowledge of God in Calvin's Theology*. New York Columbia, 1952.

Draper, Jr., James T. *Authority: The Critical Issue for Southern Baptists*. Old Tappan, New Jersey: Fleming H. Revell Company, 1984.

Dyrness, William. *Themes in Old Testament Theology*. Downers Grove, Illinois: Inter-Varsity, 1979.

Egner, David. *The Case for the Perfectly Good Book: The Bible*. Grand Rapids, Michigan: William B. Eerdmans Company, 1978.

Evans, William. *The Great Doctrines of the Bible.* Chicago, Illinois: Moody Press, 1973.

Fackre, Gabriel. *The Christian Story*. Grand Rapids, Michigan: William B. Eerdmans Company, 1988.

Forbush, William B., ed. *Fox's Book of Martyrs.* Tenth ed. Grand Rapids, Michigan: Zondervan Publishing Company, 1975.

France, R.T. *Jesus and the Old Testament.* Grand Rapids, Michigan: Baker Book House, 1982.

——————. *The Evidence for Jesus.* Downers Grove, Illinois: Inter-Varsity, 1986.

Free, Joseph P., and Howard F. Vos. *Archaeology and Bible History.* Grand Rapids, Michigan: Zondervan Publishing Company, 1992.

Fuller, Reginald H., and Ernest Wright. *The Book of the Acts of God.* Garden City, New York: Doubleday and, 1957.

Gaebelein, Frank E., ed. *The Expositor's Bible Commentary.* First ed. Vol. 1. Grand Rapids, Michigan: Zondervan, 1979.

Graham, Billy. *Just As I Am.* Grand Rapids, Michigan: Zondervan Company, 1997.

——————. *The Holy Spirit.* Minneapolis, MN: Billy Graham Evangelistic Association, 1991.

Geisler, Norman. *Christ: The Theme of the Bible.* Chicago, Illinois: Moody P, 1968.

——————. *Christian Apologetics.* Grand Rapids, Michigan: Baker Book House, 1976.

Glueck, Nelson. *Rivers in the Desert: History of Negev.* New York: Farrar, Straus, and Cadahy, 1959.

Guthrie, Donald. *New Testament Theology.* Downers Grove, Illinois: Inter-Varsity P, 1981.

Guthrie, Donald. *The Historical and Literary Criticism of The News Testament*. Grand Rapids, Michigan: Zondervan Company, 1979.

Harrop, Clayton. *History of the New Testament in Plain Language*. Waco, Texas: Word Books, 1984.

Hastings, H.L. *Will the Old Book Stand?* Boston: Scriptural Tract Repository, 1890.

Hick, John. *Philosophy of Religion*. Englewood Cliffs, New Jersey: Prentice-Hall, Inc., 1963.

Hornor, Noel. *Is The Bible True?* Cincinnati, Ohio: United Church of God, 2008.

Hovey, Alvah. *Manual of Systematic Theology and Christian Ethics*. Boston, MA: Henry P. Young and Company, 1877.

Hume, David. *An Inquiry Concerning Human Understanding*. New York: C.H. Hendel edition, 1955.

Hume, David. *The Natural History of Religion*. Stanford: H.E. Root edition, 1957.

Jackson, Jeremy C. *No Other Foundation.* Westchester, Illinois: Cornerstone, 1980.

James, Fannie B. *Truth and Health*. Denver: W.F. Robinson Printing Company, 1911.

Jefferson, Thomas. *The Jefferson Bible*. Boston: Beacon Press, 1989.

Jeremiah, David. *The Handwriting on the Wall.* Dallas, Texas: Word, 1992.

Jewett, Paul K. *Emil Brunner: An introduction to the Man and His Thought.* Chicago: Inter-Varsity Press, 1961.

Johnson, Roger A. and Ernest Wallwork. *Critical Issues in Modern Religion.* Englewood Cliffs, New Jersey: Prentice-Hall, Inc., 1973.

Kaufman, Gordan D. *Systematic Theology: A Historicist Perspective.* New York: Charles Scribner's Sons, 1968.

Kelso, James L. *An Archaeologist Looks at the Bible.* Waco, Texas: Word, 1969.

King James Bible. Nashville, TN: Holman Bible, 1973.

Lane, Dennis T. Editor. *Letters of Francis A. Schaeffer.* Westchester, Illinois: Crossway Books, 1985.

Latourette, Kenneth S. *A History of Christianity.* New York: Harper and Row, 1953.

Lea, John W. *The Greatest Book in the World.* Philadelphia: n.p., 1929.

Lewis, C.S. *Mere Christianity.* New York: The MacMillian Company, 1960.

Lightfoot, Neil R. *How We Got the Bible.* Grand Rapids, Michigan: Baker Book House, 1963.

Lindsell, Harold. *God's Incomparable Word.* Minneapolis, Minnesota: Billy Graham Evangelistic Association, 1977.

Lindsell, Harold. *The Battle For The Bible.* Grand Rapids, Michigan: Zondervan Company, 1976.

Lindsell, Harold. *The New Paganism.* San Francisco, CA: Harper & Row, 1987.

Livingston, James C. *Modern Christian Thought*. New York, New York: The MacMillan Company, 1971.

Lockyer, Herbert. *All the Messianic Prophecies of the Bible*. Grand Rapids, Michigan: Zondervan Publishing House, 1973.

Lockyer, Herbert. *Everything Jesus Taught*. *Vol. One*. New York: Harper & Row, 1976.

McDowell, Josh and Bill Wilson. *He Walked Among Us*. San Bernardino, California: Here's Life, 1988

McDowell, Josh, comp. *More Evidence that Demands a Verdict*. Van Nuys, California: Campus Crusade for Christ International, 1975.

_____. *New Evidence That Demands a Verdict*. Nashville, Tennessee: Thomas Nelson, 1999.

_____. *The Guide to Understanding the Bible*. San Bernardino, California: Here's Life, Inc., 1984.

_____. *He Walked Among Us*. San Bernardino, CA: Here's Life, 1988.

_____. *More Than A Carpenter*. Minneapolis, Minnesota: World Wide Publications, 1977.

Mead, Frank, ed. *The Encyclopedia of Religious Quotations*. Westwood, Illinois: Fleming H. Revell, n.d.

Metzger, Bruce, ed. *The Apocrypha*. New York: Oxford University Press, 1965.

Mickelsen, A. Berkeley. *Better Study the Bible*. Glendale, California: G/L Publications, 1977.

Montgomery, John Warwick. *Faith Founded on Fact*. New York, New York: Thomas Nelson Inc., 1978.

Moody, Dale. *The Word of Truth*. Grand Rapids, Michigan: William B. Eerdmans Company, 1981.

Moreland, J.P. and Michael j. Wilkins. Gen Ed. *Jesus Under Fire*. Grand Rapids, Michigan: Zondervan Publishing House, 1995.

New King James Bible: New Testament. Nashville: Thomas Nelson, 1979.

Paine, Thomas. *The Age of Reason*. Paris: Barrois, 1794, 1795, 1807.

Packer, J.I. *Fundamentalism and the Word of God*. Grand Rapids, Michigan: William B. Eerdmans Publishing Company, 1958.

Pinnock, Clark. *Set Forth Your Case*. New Jersey: Craig Press, 1968.

Placher, William C. *Unapologetic Theology*. Louisville, Kentucky: John Knox, 1989.

Ramsey, William. *Was Jesus Born in Bethlehem?* Minneapolis, MN: James Family Printing Company, 1978.

_____. *The Bearing of Recent Discovery on the Trustworthiness of the New Testament*. London: Hodder and Stoughton, 1915.

Reese, Ed. *The Life and Ministry of George Mueller*. Glenwood, Illinois: Fundamental, 1975.

_____. *The Life and Ministry of Reuben Torrey*. Glenwood, Illinois: Fundamental, 1975.

_____. *The Life and Ministry of Mel Trotter*. Glenwood, Illinois: Fundamental, 1975.

Rice, John R., comp. *A Coffer of Jewels: The Bible*. Murfreesboro, Tennessee: Sword of the Lord, 1963.

Rimmer, Harry. *Seven Wonders of the Wonderful Word*. Grand Rapids, Michigan: William B. Eerdmans Company, 1943.

Sabiers, Karl. *Mathematics Prove Holy Scriptures*. Los Angeles: Tell International, 1941.

Schaff, Philip. *History of the Christian Church*. Grand Rapids, Michigan: William B. Eerdmans Publishing Company, 1962.

Schaeffer, Francis A. *A Christian Manifesto*. Westchester, Illinois: Crossway Books, 1982.

_____. *The Person of Christ*. New York: American Tract Society, 1913.

_____. *Escape From Reason*. Downers Grove, Illinois: Inter-Varsity Press, 1968.

Schroeder, H.J. *Canons and Decrees of the Council of Trent*. St. Louis, MO: Hender, 1950.

Shindler, Robert. *The Life and Labors of Charles Haddon Spurgeon*. New York: A.C. Armstrong and Son, 1892.

Simmons, Paul D. *Issues in Christian Ethics*. Nashville, Tennessee: Broadman, 1980.

Stott, John R.W. *Understanding the Bible*. Grand Rapids, Michigan: Zondervan Company, 1984.

Strong, Augustus H. *Systematic Theology*. Valley Forge, PA: Judson Press, 1907.

Warfield, Benjamin. *Calvin and Augustine.* Philadelphia: Presbyterian and Reformed, 1956.

Whiston, William, trans. *Complete Works of Josephus.* Grand Rapids, Michigan: Kregel Publications, 1970.

Wilson, Robert Dick. *Is the Higher Criticism Scholarly?* Philadelphia, PA: The Sunday School Times Company, 1922.

Wood, Skevington. *Captive to the Word.* Grand Rapids, Michigan: William B. Eerdmans Company, 1969.

Youngblood, Ronald. *The Heart of the Old Testament.* Grand Rapids: Baker Book House, 1971.

LECTURE:

Newman, Stewart. "Metaphysics." (in class course lecture, Campbell University, Buies Creek, NC, Fall Semester, 1973).

PERIODICALS:

Kay, James F. "Theological Table-Talk Myth or Narrative: Bultmann's New Testament and Mythology." *Theology Today* XLVIII (October, 1991): 326–32.

Panin, Ivan. "Inspiration of the Scriptures Scientifically Demonstrated," letter in *The New York Sun.* November 19, 1899

REFERENCES WORKS:

A Ready Reference History of the English Bible. New York: American Bible
    Society, 1976.

Archer, Gleason L. *Encyclopedia of Bible Difficulties.* Grand Rapids,
    Michigan: Zondervan Publishing House, 1982.

Calvin, John. *Institutes of the Christian Religion.* Vol. II. Trans. Henry
    Beveridge. London: James Clarke & Co., 1953.

Elwell, Walter A. *Evangelical Dictionary of Theology.* Grand Rapids,
    Michigan: Baker Book House Company, 2009.

Henry, Carl H. "Special Revelation." *Barker's Dictionary of Theology.*
    Grand Rapids, Michigan: Baker Book House, 1960. 457-58.

Livingstone, E.A., ed. *The Concise Oxford Dictionary of the Christian
    Church.* Great Britain: Oxford UP, 1977.

Marty, Martin E., and Dean G. Peerman, eds. *A Handbook of Christian
    Theologians.* New York: Word Company, 1965.

Sweeting, George, Complier. *Great Quotes and Illustrations.* Waco, Texas:
    Word Books Publishers, 1985.

Tenney, Merrill, Gen. Ed. *Pictorial Bible Dictionary.* Nashville, Tennessee:
    The Southwestern Company, 1966.

Voorwinde, Steven. *Wisdom for Today's Issues.* Phillipsburg, New Jersey:
    Presbyterian and Reformed Publishing Company, 1981.

WEBSITES:

Broadus, John A. "The Ethical Teachings of Jesus." *Elbourne.org.* Jesus of Nazareth, n.d. http://elbourne.org/baptist/broadus/jesus/ jesus_broadus_02.html. (accessed May 6, 2011).

Broadus, John A. "The Personal Character of Jesus." *Elbourne.org.* Jesus of Nazareth, n.d. <http://elbourne.org/baptist/broadus/jesus/ jesus_broadus_01.html>. (accessed May 6, 2011).

Celsus. *A True Discourse. "Celsus—Thrice Holy Library."* Thrice Holy Library, n.d. Web. <http://triceholy.net/Texts/Celsus.html>. (accessed March 30, 2011).

Crosby, Jonathan. "Thus Saith the Lord." *Let God Be True.* The Church of Greenville, no date. <http://www.letgodbetrue.com/sermons/ pdf/thus-saith-the-lord.pdf>. (accessed March 22, 2011).

Geisler, Norman. Ankerberg Theological Research Institute.org. Baker Encyclopedia of Christian Apologetics pdf. "Biblical Criticism." 1999. http://ankerberg.com/Articles/ PDFArchives/ theoogical-dictionary/TD1W0101.pdf. (accessed March 20, 2011).

"Great Moral Teacher?" *Jesusmystery.com.* Ed. Larry Chapman. Y-Jesus Magazine, n.d. http://www.jesusmystery.com/article. php?sec=3&arc=2# (accessed May 7, 2011).

Jones, Grant. "The Septuagint in the New Testament." *Notes on the Septuagint.* Robert Jones, 2000. Web. <http://mysite.verizon. net/rgjones3/index.html>. (accessed March 30, 2011).

Mike Magee, "What Matters Most, Christ's Resurrection or His Moral Teachings?" (*Mike Mageeword.press.com.* Word Press, April 30, 2011). <http://mikemagee.wordpress.com/2011/04/30/what-

matter-most-christs-resurrection-or-his-moral-teaching/>. (accessed May 7, 2011).

Moorehead, William G. "The Moral Glory of Jesus Christ, a Proof of Inspiration." *Xmission.com*. Fundamentals: A Testimony to the Truth, 22 Dec. 2005. <http://www.xmission.com/~fidelis/volume2/chapter3/moorehead.php>. (accessed May 6, 2011).

Moreland, J.P. *"How Did Jesus Act?: Jesus as a Moral Teacher."* The Scriptorium, August 13, 2007. http://www.scriptoriumdaily.com/2007/08/13/how-did-jesus-act-jesus-as-a-moral-teacher/. (accessed June 7, 2011).

Murawski, John. "Biblical Writers Intended to Deceive, Ehrman Says." *www.newsobserve.com*. 6 Feb. 2011. Web. (accessed April 10, 2011).

Pink, Arthur W. "Introduction to Divine Inspiration of the Bible." E-Sword. www.bible.org. 2011. (accessed March 13, 2011).

Price, Robert M. "Taking up Schleiermacher's Challenge to the Canon." Theological Publications. 2009. <http://www.robertmprice.mindvendor.com/art_takingup_schleierm_challenge.htm>. (accessed March 28, 2011).

"Quotes About Jesus." (*Tentmaker.org*. Ed. Gary Amirault. FreeFind, 2010), <http://www.tentmaker.org/store/about-us/info_1.html>. (accessed May 7, 2011).

Seiglie, Mario. "Can You Prove the Bible is True?" The Good News. 2011. www.gnmagazine.org. 2011. The Good News. (accessed March 30, 2011).

Thompson, Bert. "In Defense of the Bible's Inspiration." Apologetics Press. 1999. www.apologeticspress.org. (accessed April 13, 2011).

Endnotes

WHO IS RIGHT?

1   David Hume, *The Natural History of Religion* (Stanford: H.E. Root edition, 1957), 75.

2   —————, An *Inquiry Concerning Human Understanding* (New York: C.H. Hendel Edition, 1955), 139-140.

3   See Thomas Paine, *The Age of Reason* (Paris: Barrois, 1794, 1795, 1807).

4   *Ecce Homo, in the Portable Nietzsche,* Walter Kaufmann, trans. (New York: Vintage, 1960), 21.

5   James C. Livingston, *Modern Christian Thought* (New York: MacMillan Company, 1971), 196.

6   *The Birth of Tragedy, in the Portable Nietzsche, Walter Kaufmann,* trans. (New York: Vintage, 1960), 23.

7   Livingston, 202.

8   Ibid., 195.

9   Friedrich Schleiermacher, *The Christian Faith, Vol. II* (New York: Harper & Row, 1963), p. 591.

10   Ibid., 593.

11   Ibid., 596.

12   Soren Kierkegaard, *Concluding Unscientific Postscript* (New Jersey: Princeton, 1941). 182.

13   Ibid., 181.

14   Livingston, 374.

15 Martin E. Marty and Dean G. Peerman, eds., *Handbook of Christian Theologians* (New York: The Word Publishing Company, 1965), 445.

16 Kay, James F. "Theological Table-Talk Myth or Narrative: Bultmann's New Testament and Mythology" *Theology Today* XLVIII (Science Press: Ephrata, PA October, 1991), 327.

17 Calvin, John. *Institutes of the Christian Religion, Vol. II*, Trans. Henry Beveridge (London: James Clarke & Co., 1953), 1:7:4 & 5.

18 Ibid., 1:7:4.

19 Ibid., 4:8:9.

20 Benjamin Warfield, *Calvin and Augustine* (Philadelphia: Presbyterian and Reformed Publishing Company, 1956), 49.

21 Calvin, *Institutes,* 2:10:7.

22 Lane T. Dennis, ed., *Letters of Francis A. Schaeffer* (Westchester, Illinois: Crossway Books, 1985), 72.

23 Ibid., 82.

24 Ibid., 104.

25 Francis A. Schaeffer, *Escape From Reason* (Downers Grove, Illinois: Inter-Varsity Press, 1968), 84-94.

26 Schaeffer, 89-90.

27 Billy Graham, *The Holy Spirit* (Minneapolis, MN: Billy Graham Evangelistic Association, 1991), 39-42.

28 Ibid., 42.

29 Ibid.

30 Ibid., 44.

THE BIBLE'S CLAIM

31 Harold Lindsell, *The New Paganism* (San Francisco: Harper and Row Publishers), 177.

32 *Baker's Dictionary of Theology*, "Special Revelation," Carl H. Henry (Grand Rapids, Michigan: Baker book House, 1960), 457.

33 David S. Dockery, *The Doctrine of the Bible* (Nashville, Tennessee: Seminary Extension, 1984), 13.

34 Harold Lindsell, *God's Incomparable Word* (Minneapolis, Minnesota: Billy Graham Association, 1977), 21.

35 Augustus H. Strong, *Systematic Theology* (Valley Forge, Pa: Judson Press, 1907), 113.

36 Francis A. Schaeffer, *Escape From Reason* (Downers Grove, Illinois: Inter-Varsity Press, 1968), 89.

37 Dale Moody, *The Word of Truth* (Grand Rapid, Michigan: William B. Eerdmans Publishing Company, 1981), 40-41.

38 David Egner, *The Case for the Perfectly Good Book, the Bible* (Grand Rapids, Michigan: Radio Bible Class, 1978), 10.

39 Billy Graham, *The Holy Spirit* (Waco, Texas: Word Books Publisher, 1978), 42.

40 Strong, 204.

41 John R. Rice, complier, *A Coffer of Jewels: The Bible* (Murfreesboro, Tennessee: Sword of the Lord Publishers, 1963), 161.

42 James T. Draper, Jr., *Authority: Critical Issue for Southern Baptists* (Old Tappan, New Jersey: Fleming H. Revell Company, 1984), 81.

43 Rice, 256.

44 Ibid., 152.

45 George Duncan Barry, *The Inspiration and Authority of the Holy Scripture: A Study in the Literature of the First Five Centuries* (New York: MacMillian, 1919), 140

46 Egner, 55.

47 Frank E. Gaebelein, General Editor, *The Expositor's Bible Commentary, Vol. I,* "The Authority and Inspiration of the Bible," Carl Henry (Grand Rapids, Michigan: Zondervan Publishing House, 1979), 25.

48 Draper, 89.

49 Alvah Hovey, *Manual of Systematic Theology and Christian Ethics* (Boston, MA: Henry B. Young and Company, 1877), 83, 85.

50 Norman Geisler, *Christian Apologetics* (Grand Rapids, Michigan: Baker Book House, p. 1976), 362.

51 Draper, 59.

52 Rice, 162-163.

53 B.H. Carroll, *Inspiration of the Bible* (New York: Revell, 1930), 20.

54 J.I. Packer, *Fundamentalism and the Word of God* (Grand Rapids, Michigan: William B. Eerdmans Publishing Company, 1982), 47.

55   Graham, *Holy Spirit*, 43.

56   Harold Lindsell, *The Battle for the Bible* (Grand Rapids, Michigan: Zondervan Publishing Company, 1976), 39.

57   Packer., 68.

CAN WE GET A WITNESS?

58   Norman Geisler, *Christian Apologetics* (Grand Rapids, Michigan: Baker Book House, 1976), 368.

59   Herbert Lockyer, *Everything Jesus Taught, Volume I* (San Francisco: Harper and Row Publishers, 1976), 49.

60   Billy Graham, *The Holy Spirit* (Waco, Texas: Word Books Publishers, 1978), 42.

61   John R. Rice, complier, *A Coffer of Jewels: The Bible* (Murfreesboro, Tennessee: Sword of the Lord Publishers, 1963), 167.

62   Harold Lindsell, *God's Incomparable Word* (Minneapolis, Minnesota: Billy Graham Evangelistic Association, 1977), 37-38.

63   John Calvin, *Institutes of the Christian Religion, Vol. II*, Trans. Henry Beveridge (London: James Clarke & Co., 1953), 1:7:4&5.

64   Josephus, *Contra Apion*, 1:8.

65   Ibid.

66   Brooke Foss Westcott. "On the Primitive Doctrine of Inspiration," In *The Bible in the Early Church*, ed. Everett Ferguson, David Scholer and Paul Corby Finney, III (New York: Garland, 1993), 25.

67   David Egner, *The Case for a Perfectly Good Book, the Bible* (Grand Rapids, Michigan: Radio Bible Class, 1978), 39.

68   Ibid., 49-50.

69   Edward. A. Dowey, Jr., *The Knowledge of God in Calvin's Theology* (New York: Columbia, 1952), 109.

70   W.J. McGlothlin, *Baptist Confessions of Faith*, (Philadelphia: American Baptist Publication Society, 1911), 91.

71   Ibid., 119.

72   Russell H. Conwell, *The Life of Charles Haddon Spurgeon* (Edgewood Publishing Company, 1892), 574-576.

73   Augustus H. Strong, *Systematic Theology* (Valley Forge, PA: Judson Press, 1907), 196.

74 Rice, 9-10.

75 J.I. Packer, *Fundamentalism and the Word of God* (Grand Rapids, Michigan: William B. Eerdmans Publishing Company, 1958), 95, 113-114, 169.

THEMATIC UNITY AFFIRMS BIBLE'S INSPIRATION

76 Augustus H. Strong, *Systematic Theology* (Valley Forge, PA: Judson Press, 1907), 175.

77 Ronald Youngblood, *The Heart of the Old Testament* (Grand Rapids: Baker Book House, 1971), 9.

78 Frank E. Gaebelein, General Editor, *The Expositor's Bible Commentary, Volume I* (Grand Rapids, Michigan: Zondervan Publishing Company, 1979), 461.

79 Strong, 178-179.

80 J.I Packer, *Fundamentalism and the Word of God* (Grand Rapids, Michigan: William B. Eerdmans Publishing Company, 1958), 84-85.

81 Norman Geisler, *Christ: The Theme of the Bible* (Chicago, Illinois: Moody Press, 1968), 110.

MATHEMATICAL UNITY AFFIRMS BIBLE'S INSPIRATIOIN

82 From a pamphlet by Irwin Publishing Inc. 180 West Beaver Creek Road, Richmond Hill, Ontario L4B 1B4, Canada.

83 Karl Sabiers, *Mathematics Prove Holy Scriptures* (Los Angeles: Tell International, 1941), 113.

84 Ibid., 27

85 Ibid., 78.

86 Ibid., 64.

87 Ivan Panin, "Inspiration of the Scriptures Scientifically Demonstrated," letter in *The New York Sun* (November 19, 1899).

88 Keith L. Brooks, *Overwhelming Mathematical Evidence of the Divine Inspiration of the Scriptures* (Syracuse, New York: Book Fellowship, n.d.), 4.

89 Sabiers, 63.

FULFILLED PROPHECY AFFIRMS BIBLE'S INSPIRATION

90 Herbert Lockyer, *All the Messianic Prophecies of the Bible* (Grand Rapids, Michigan: Zondervan Publishing House, 1973), 11.

91 Ibid., 9.

92 Ibid., 11.

93 Augustus H. Strong, *Systematic Theology* (Valley Forge, PA: Judson Press, 1907), 134.

94 Strong, 137.

95 Lockyer, 17.

96 Ibid., 64.

97 Ibid., 50.

ARCHAEOLOGY AFFIRMS BIBLE'S INSPIRATION

98 Frank E. Gaebelein, General Editor, *Expositor's Bible Commentary* (Grand Rapids Michigan: Zondervan Publishing House, 1979), 309.

99 Ibid.

100 James L. Kelso, *An Archaeologist Looks at the Gospels* (Waco, Texas: Word Books Publishers, 1969), 1.

101 Gabelein, 31.

102 Nelson Glueck, *Rivers in the Desert: History of Negev* (New York: Farrar, Straus, and Cadahy, 1959), 31.

103 Robert D. Wilson, *Is the Higher Criticism Scholarly?* (Philadelphia, Pa: The Sunday School Times Company, 1911), 10.

104 Lindsell, Incomparable, 46.

105 Wilson, p. 15

106 Gleason L. Archer, *Encyclopedia of Bible Difficulties* (Grand Rapids, Michigan: Zondervan Publishing House, 1982). 52.

107 Ibid., 53

108 Wilson, 15.

109 Joseph P. Free and Howard F. Vos, *Archaeology and Bible History* (Grand Rapids, Michigan: Zondervan Publishing House, 1992), 45.

110 John Elder, *Prophets, Idols, and Diggers* (New York: bobs-Merrill Co., 1960), 75.

111 Fred H. Wright, *Highlights of Archaeology in Bible Lands* (Chicago: Moody, 1955), 94-95.

112 Free and Vos, 78.

113 Ibid., 111.

114 Wilson, 18-19.

115 Ibid., 19-20.

116 John R. Rice, *A Coffer of Jewels: The Bible* (Murfreesboro, Tennessee: Sword of the Lord Publishers, 1963), 214.

117 Ibid.

118 Free and Vos, 201

119 Rice., 215

120 Gaebelein, 403.

121 William Ramsay, *The Bearing of Recent Discovery on the Trustworthiness of the New Testament* (London: Hodder and Stoughton, 1915), 222.

122 William Ramsey, *Was Jesus Born in Bethlehem?* (Minneapolis, MN: James Family Printing Company, 1978), 14-16.

123 Lindsell, *Incomparable*, 47.

124 Gaebelein, 669.

125 R.T. France, *The Evidence for Jesus* (Downers Grove, Illinois: Inter-Varsity, 1986), 5.

126 Josh McDowell, *He Walked Among Us* (San Bernardino, CA: Here's Life, 1988), 215.

127 J.P. Morland and Michael J. Wilkins, gen. eds., *Jesus Under Fire,* (Grand Rapids, Michigan: Zondervan Publishing House, 1995), 40-41.

128 Free and Vos, 256.

129 Ibid, 1.

130 Clark Pinnock, *Set Forth Your Case* (New Jersey: Craig Press, 1968), 58.

131 Free and Vos, 13-14.

132 Archer, *Difficulties*, 11-12.

133 Bruce Metzger, Editor, *The Apocrypha* (New York: Oxford University Press, 1965), 223.

134 William Whiston, Translator, *Complete Works of Josephus* (Grand Rapids, Michigan: Kregel Publications, 1970), 257.

135 William Byron Forbush, Editor, *Fox's Book of Martyrs* (Grand Rapids, Michigan: Zondervan Publishing House, 1975), 24.

136 Harry Rimmer, *Seven Wonders of the Wonderful Word* (Grand Rapids, Michigan: William B. Eerdmans Publishing Company, 1943), 15.

137 John R. Rice, *A Coffer of Jewels: The Bible* (Murfreesboro, Tennessee: Sword of the Lord Publishers, 1963), 119.

138 H.J. Schroeder, *Canons and Decrees of the Council of Trent* (St. Louis, MO: Hender, 1950), 274.

139 Forbush, 87-134.

140 Ibid., 143.

141 Skevington Wood, *Captive to the Word* (Grand Rapids, Michigan: William B. Eerdmans Publishing Company, 1969), 72.

142 Clayton Harrop, *History of the New Testament in Plain Language* (Waco, Texas: Word Books, 1984), 142.

143 Celsus, *A True Discourse* (Thrice Holy Library, n.d.) http://thriceholy.net/Texts/Celsus.html (accessed March 30, 2011).

144 H.L. Hastings, *Will the Old Book Stand?* (Boston: Scriptural Tract Repository, 1890), 5.

145 Ibid.

146 H.L. Hastings, *Will the Old Book Stand?*, 5. See also Josh McDowell, *The New Evidence That Demands a Verdict* (Nashville: Thomas Nelson Publishing, 1999), 11.

147 Bert Thompson, "In Defense of the Bible's Inspiration" (Apologetics Press, 1999). http://www.apologeticspress.org/apcontent.aspx?category=13&article=1330 (accessed April 13, 2011).

148 Sidney Collett, *All About the Bible* (Grand Rapids, Michigan: Fleming H. Revell, 1972), 72.

149 Livingston, 1.

150 Norman Geisler, *Christian Apologetics* (Grand Rapids, Michigan: Baker book House, 1976), 29.

151 William C. Placher, *Unapologetic Theology* (Louisville, Kentucky: John Knox Press, 1989), 25.

152 Livingston, 3.

153 Jacques Choron, *The Romance of Philosophy* (New York, New York: The MacMillan Company, 1963), 118.

154 John Murawski, "Biblical Writers Intended to deceive, Ehrman says" (www.newsobserver.com, February 6, 2011) http://www.newsobserver.com/2011/02/06/968376/bible-writers-intended-to-deceive.html (accessed April 10, 2011).

155 Ibid.

156 John W. Lea, *The Greatest Book in the World*, (Philadelphia: n.p., 1929), 17-18.

PRACTICALITY FOR LIVING AFFIRMS BIBLE'S INSPIRATION

157 Peter Craigie, *The Problem of War in the Old Testament* (Grand Rapids, Michigan: William B. Eerdmans Publishing Company, 1978), 96-97.

158 Augustus H. Strong, *Systematic Theology* (Valley Forge, PA: Judson Press, 1907), 178.

159 Thomas Jefferson, *The Jefferson Bible* (Boston: Beacon Press, 1989), vi-x.

160 John R. Rice, *A Coffer of Jewels: The Bible* (Murfreesboro, Tennessee: Sword of the Lord Publishers, 1963), 291.

161 Ibid.

162 David Barton, *Original Intent* (Aledo, Texas: Wallbuilders Press, 1996), 137.

163 Rice, 138.

164 Ibid.

165 Nancy DeMoss, ed., *The Rebirth of America* (Philadelphia: Arthur S. DeMoss, 1986), 29.

166 DeMoss, 33.

167 Strong, 186.

[168] Paul Simmons, ed., *Issues in Christian Ethics* (Nashville, Tennessee: Broadman Press, 1980), 21, 34.

[169] Strong, 178-179.

MORAL LIFE OF JESUS AFFIRMS BIBLE INSPIRATION

[170] Josephus, *Antiquities*, 18:63-64.

[171] Mike Magee, "What Matters Most, Christ's Resurrection or His Moral Teachings?" *Mike Mageeword.press.com*. Word Press, April 30, 2011, <http://mikemagee.wordpress.com/2011/04/30/what-matter-most-christs-resurrection-or-his-moral-teaching/>. (May 7, 2011).

[172] Fannie B. James, *Truth and Health* (Denver: W.F. Robinson Printing Company, 1911), 174.

[173] Fyodor Dostoevsky, The *Brothers Karamazov,* trans. Constance Garnett (New York: Signet Classic Printing, 1958), 312.

[174] "Great Moral Teacher?" *Jesusmystery.com*. Ed. Larry Chapman. Y-Jesus Magazine, n.d. http://www.jesusmystery.com/article.php?sec=3&arc=2# (May 7, 2011).

[175] James C. Livingston, *Modern Christian Thought*_(New York: The Macmillan Company, 1971), 199.

[176] Robert H. Culpepper, *Interpreting the Atonement* (Grand Rapids, Michigan: William B. Eerdmans Publishing Company, 1966), 91.

[177] Johnston Ross, *The Universality of Jesus* (New York: Fleming H. Revell, 1906), 146.

[178] John A. Broadus. "The Personal Character of Jesus." *Elbourne.org*. Jesus of Nazareth, n.d., <http://elbourne.org/baptist/broadus/jesus/jesus_broadus_01.html>. (accessed May 6, 2011).

[179] Frank Mead, ed. *The Encyclopedia of Religious Quotations* (Westwood, Illinois: Fleming H. Revell, n.d.), 49.

[180] J.P. Moreland. *How Did Jesus Act?: Jesus as a Moral Teacher*, The Scriptorium, August 13, 2007. http://www.scriptoriumdaily.com/2007/08/13/how-did-jesus-act-jesus-as-a-moral-teacher/ (accessed June 7, 2011).

[181] Josh McDowell, *More Than a Carpenter* (Minneapolis, Minnesota: World Wide Publications, 1977), 15.

[182] C.S. Lewis, *Mere Christianity* (New York: The MacMillian Company, 1960), 40-41.

[183] William G. Moorehead, "The Moral Glory of Jesus Christ, a Proof of Inspiration." *Xmission.com*. Fundamentals: A Testimony to the Truth, 22 Dec. 2005. <http://www.xmission.com/~fidelis/volume2/chapter3/moorehead.php>. (accessed May 6, 2011).

[184] Ibid.

[185] Philip Schaff, *The Person of Christ* (New York: American Tract Society, 1913), 94-95.

[186] Alvah Hovey, *Manual of Systematic Theology and Christian Ethics* (Boston, MA: Henry A. Young and Company, 1877), 53-54.

[187] Ibid., 66-67.

[188] Philip Schaff, *History of the Christian Church* (Grand Rapids, Michigan: William B. Eerdmans Publishing Company, 1962), 109.

[189] Schaff, 109.

[190] Kenneth S. Latourette, *A History of Christianity* (New York: Harper and Row, 1953), 44, 48.

[191] H.L. Hastings, *Will the Old Book Stand?* (Boston: Scriptural Tract Repository, 1890), 5.

[192] Augustus H. Strong, *Systematic Theology* (Valley Forge, PA: Judson Press, 1907), 190.

[193] John A Broadus. "The Ethical Teachings of Jesus" (*Elbourne.org*. Jesus of Nazareth, n.d), http://elbourne.org/baptist/broadus/jesus/jesus_broadus_02.html, (accessed May 6, 2011).

[194] Hovey, 67.

[195] Strong, 189.

[196] Harvie Branscomb, *The Teachings of Jesus* (New York: Abingdon Press, 1959), 89.

[197] Strong, 190.

[198] Moorehead, "The Moral Glory of Jesus."

199 Augustus H. Strong, *Systematic Theology* (Valley Forge, PA: Judson Press, 1907), 131.

200 Augustine, translated by R.S. Pine-Coffin, *The Confessions of Saint Augustine* (New York: Penguin Group, 1961), Book VIII, Paragraphs 28 and 29.

201 Skevington Wood, *Captive to the Lord* (Grand Rapids, Michigan: William B. Eerdmans Publishing Company, 1969), 53.

202 Ibid., 72.

203 Robert Shindler, *The Life and Labors of Charles Haddon Spurgeon*, (New York: A.C. Armstrong and Son, 1892), 35–36.

204 Ibid., 305.

205 Ed Reece, *The Life and Ministry of George Mueller* (Glenwood, Illinois: Fundamental Publishers, 1975), 4.

206 Ibid., 10.

207 Strong, 813–814.

208 Ed Reese, *The Life and Ministry of Reuben Torrey* (Glenwood, Illinois: Fundamental Publishers, 1975), 4.

209 Ed Reese, *The Life and Ministry of Mel Trotter* (Glenwood, Illinois: Fundamental Publishers, 1975), 4.

210 Ibid., 7.

211 Billy Graham, *Just As I Am*, (San Francisco: Zondervan, 1997), 3.

CONCLUSION

212 John W. Montgomery, *Faith Founded on Fact* (Thomas Nelson Publishers: Nashville, Tennessee, 1978), xx.

213 Stewart Newman, "Metaphysics" (in class course lecture, Campbell University, Buies Creek, NC, Fall Semester, 1973).

214 Norman Geisler, *Christian Apologetics* (Grand, Michigan: Baker Book House, 1976), 48.

215 Ibid., 22, 133–134.

216 Paul K. Jewett, *Emil Brunner: An introduction to the Man and His Thought* (Chicago: Inter-Varsity Press, 1961), 32.

217 Ibid., 32–33.

[218] J.I Packer, *Fundamentalism and the Word of God* (Grand Rapids, Michigan: William B. Eerdmans Publishing Company, 1958), 128.

[219] Ibid., 143.

[220] Alvah Hovey, *Manual of Systematic Theology and Christian Ethics* (Boston, MA: Henry A. Young and Company, 1877), 12-13.

[221] Augustus H. Strong, *Systematic Theology* (Valley Forge, PA: Judson Press, 1907), 2-3.

[222] Geisler, 376-377.

[223] Strong, 770.

CPSIA information can be obtained at www.ICGtesting.com
Printed in the USA
BVOW031205250911

271933BV00001B/6/P

9 781462 706372